natural English

intermediate student's book

Ruth Gairns & Stuart Redman

OXFORD

UNIVERSITY PRESS

contents

in **unit four** ...

joke the kangaroo

natural English
expressing a preference
asking for repetition
expressing interest
saying how much you know
phone greetings

grammar & vocabulary
modal verbs *would, could / might*
uses of *will*
facial actions
food and drink
TV programmes

wordbooster
phrases expressing your opinion
synonyms

speaking
role play a conversation in a café
talk about programmes you like
describe how you'd change TV programmes
how to ... make a phone call

listening
joke: *the kangaroo*
people choosing TV documentaries:
  tune in, listen carefully, listening challenge
somebody inviting a speaker to give a talk
listening booklet listening and
  pronunciation exercises

reading & writing
All I want is a burger / cup of tea
a programme of talks
complete an e-mail confirming arrangements
write a description of a talk

extended speaking
a weekend English course
Decide on talks and speakers for a weekend
course programme. Then role play a phone
conversation with one of the speakers.

test yourself! on unit four

in **unit five** ...

cartoon presents

natural English
thanking and replying
suggestions and responses
intensifying adverbs
it depends ...
generalizations (1)
giving instructions

grammar & vocabulary
adjectives and adverbs
obligation and permission: *(don't) have to,*
  must(n't), should(n't), (not) be allowed to
clothes and dressing
supermarkets

wordbooster
shopping
uses of *get*

speaking
suggest solutions for problems
talk about clothes and dressing
talk about supermarket do's and don'ts
role play giving instructions
how to ... explain what to do

listening
stories about clothes:
  tune in, listen carefully, listening challenge
instructions for working in a newsagent's
listening booklet listening and
  pronunciation exercises

reading & writing
Best behaviour: problems and solutions
pubs in Britain / bars in California
write an information sheet about bars

extended speaking
bar etiquette
Read about pubs in Britain and bars in
California. Then think about bars in your
country and produce an information sheet.

test yourself! on unit five

in **unit six** ...

joke a bad memory

natural English
giving and responding to exciting news
fortunately, hopefully, surprisingly
I don't think (that) ...
talking about advantages and disadvantages
sort, type, kind
ending a phone conversation

grammar & vocabulary
sentences with *if, when,* and *unless*
-ing form
jobs in a company
education
agreeing and disagreeing
course enquiries

wordbooster
stages in a career
learning phrases in sequences

speaking
talk about leaving school
decide how to spend a year off
discuss work issues
role play a phone conversation
how to ... enquire about a course

listening
joke: *a bad memory*
different work situations:
  tune in, listen carefully, listening challenge
a telephone enquiry
somebody describing a choice he made
listening booklet listening and
  pronunciation exercises

reading & writing
Where do we go from here?
complete an application form
a case study

extended speaking
decisions, decisions
Read the case study of a couple who have to
make an important decision. Talk about their
options and decide what they should do.
Then listen to their final decision.

test yourself! on unit six

contents

in **unit ten** …

joke three mothers

natural English
the whole …
generalizations (2)
get + past participle (passive use)
describing stereotypes
invitations
making and accepting excuses

grammar & vocabulary
articles and determiners
defining relative clauses
parties
describing character
collocation

wordbooster
reasons for being late
suffixes

speaking
talk about teenagers
describe stereotypes
discuss invitations
role play making arrangements
how to … make excuses

listening
joke: *three mothers*
people describing teenage parties
people describing their stereotypes:
  tune in, listen carefully, listening challenge
excuses and arrangements
differences between men and women
listening booklet listening and
  pronunciation exercises

reading & writing
The whole thing was a nightmare …
write invitations

extended speaking
men and women
Talk about some statements about men and
women and add your own. Then summarize
your opinions to the class

test yourself! on unit ten

in **unit eleven** …

cartoon photo booth

natural English
have (got) sth *on, with* sth *on* (= *wearing*)
giving opinions about issues
which clauses
changing plans
uses of *tell*
sequencing

grammar & vocabulary
passive forms
look, look like, look as if …
modal verbs of deduction
describing a picture

wordbooster
word building
time expressions

speaking
talk about different photos
talk about your future life story
describe paintings
how to … talk about a picture

listening
somebody describing a friend
a person's future life story:
  tune in, listen carefully, listening challenge
a real person's biography
listening booklet listening and
  pronunciation exercises

reading & writing
This is how easy it is to retouch history
write about your invented life

extended speaking
a life in pictures
Look at photos and read some information to
develop a story of somebody's life. Tell your
version and then listen to the real story.

test yourself! on unit eleven

in **unit twelve** …

joke the gold watch

natural English
What a …!
realize, remember, find out
direct speech in narrative
numbers in phrases
actually
asking for clarification

grammar & vocabulary
past perfect simple
plural nouns
driving
money

wordbooster
shopping
phrasal verbs with *back*

speaking
include details in a story
talk about pocket money
talk about clothes shopping
role play in a clothes shop
how to … say the right thing in a shop

listening
joke: *the gold watch*
stories about a lost wallet and keys:
  tune in, listen carefully, listening challenge
conversation in a clothes shop
a shopping story
listening booklet listening and
  pronunciation exercises

reading & writing
How much pocket money should you give?
a shopping story
write a shopping story for a magazine

extended speaking
shopping stories
Listen to a story about a shopping experience
and tell a story of your own. Then read
another story from a magazine and write your
own in a similar style.

test yourself! on unit twelve

welcome

lead-in

1 Order these statements in the speech bubbles above.

> I only know one or two people.
> I know practically /ˈpræktɪkli/ everyone.
> I know quite a few /kwaɪt ə ˈfjuː/ people.
> I know most people.
> ~~I know everyone.~~
> I don't know anyone at all.

2 Compare with a partner and say the statements.

3 Use the statements to tell your partner how many people you know:

1 in the class
2 in the school / college
3 in the building you live in
4 in your street
5 in your place of work / study

listen to this

tune in

1 🔊 **0.1** You're going to listen to two conversations between people who have just arrived for the first lesson of a course of evening classes. Listen to **conversation 1** and answer the questions with a partner.

1 How many speakers are there?
2 What are their names?

listen carefully

2 Listen again. Put T (true) or F (false).

1 The speakers know each other.
2 They met on a course.
3 They met two years ago.
4 The woman has a little boy.

listening challenge

3 Listen to **conversation 2**. How many speakers are there? Do they know each other?

natural English
introductions and responses

(Max), **this is** (Annie).	We already know each other.
Do you know (Annie)?	We've met before, haven't we?
Hi, I'm (Max).	Nice to meet you.
I'm really sorry, I don't remember your name.	Nice to see you.
I've forgotten your name.	

Which phrases can you use to introduce two people to each other?
Which phrase can you use when you meet someone for the first time?
Say the phrases.

4 Listen to **conversations 1** and **2**. Tick ✓ the phrases you hear in the **natural English** box.

5 Get up and talk to as many people as possible. Introduce yourself and greet others. Use the phrases from the **natural English** box.

listening booklet *p.2 for the tapescript*

it's your turn!

> Plan what you are going to say before you work with a partner.

1 **Think!** Look at the topics and choose three to talk about for thirty seconds each. Decide what you'll say, but don't write anything.

my family
  my hobbies / free time
 where I live
what I like / don't like about my home town
  how I feel about learning English
   how / where I spend my holidays
my boyfriend / girlfriend
   how I feel about my job / studies
something surprising or unusual about me
  what I'd like to happen in the future
something I believe in or feel strongly about

your own topic _____

2 Work in small groups with people you don't know very well. Take it in turns to talk about a topic and listen / ask questions.

examples Is life very expensive in Bali?
        Do you think you'll get married?
        What do you find most difficult?

3 Find a partner from a different group.

1 Which topics were easy to talk about?
2 Which were more difficult?
3 What did you find out about the other people in your group?

7

mobile invasion

life with **Agrippine**

in groups ...

Say the phrase 'mobile phone' /ˌməʊbaɪl ˈfəʊn/.

In your family, how many people have a mobile phone?
Do you often use one? Do you like them? Why/why not?

cartoon time

Read the cartoon. Do you believe the students' excuses? Why/why not?

When do you think mobile phones should be switched off?

1.1 Listen and follow the cartoon. Then test your partner on the glossary words.

 **natural English
making people listen**

You can use exclamations to get people's attention or introduce a comment. Be careful: *look* and *listen* can sometimes sound impatient.

Listen, you'll have to do it again.   **Right**, shall we go?
Look, I have to go now.   **OK**, stop that now.

Say the sentences. Underline similar examples in the cartoon.

granny Ⓖ grandmother
blood /blʌd/ red liquid in your body
urgent /ˈɜːdʒənt/ needs action now
peel (v) take the skin off fruit or vegetables
bother sb (v) disturb sb who is busy
Ⓖ this symbol means that the word/phrase is informal

9

listening small talk

vocabulary conversation topics

1 Think! How many people have you spoken to today for more than a minute? What were the conversations about?

2 Tell a partner about your conversations.

3 With a partner, complete the conversation topics below with words from the box and add two topics of your own.

current /ˈkʌrənt/	famous /ˈfeɪməs/	opposite	leisure /ˈleʒə/
gossip	events /ɪˈventz/	clothes /kləʊðz/	programmes
issues /ˈɪʃuːz/	music		

conversation topics

1 _____ activities
2 _____ affairs
3 the _____ sex
4 _____ and fashion
5 _____ about friends and family
6 sporting _____
7 pop _____
8 TV _____ and cinema
9 _____ people in the news
10 school or work-related _____

your own ideas

4 Think! Plan your answers to these questions.

1 Which of the topics in **exercise 3** do you talk about most with friends / family / colleagues?

2 Which topics do you <u>never</u> talk about, and why?

natural English
inviting people to speak 1.2

When you want to bring someone into the conversation, you can do it like this:

... yes, we often talk about fashion. **How about you, Pedro?**
... I never talk about current affairs. **What about you, Yoko?**

Listen. Then try to use these questions to make sure everyone in your group speaks.

5 Talk about your answers to **exercise 4** in small groups.

listen to this

Marcella

Nigel

Juliet

tune in

1 (1.3) You're going to listen to Marcella and Nigel describing conversations they've had.

1 Which phrases in the box do you think go with which speaker?

Marcella begins:

I was queueing up for some tickets the other day …

Nigel begins:

Oh, I was having this terrible conversation at work yesterday …

> a motorbike courier
> he's just got engaged
> Malcolm from the Accounts Department
> find my way somewhere
> look at his (London) A to Z
> Angela, who's my supervisor

2 Listen and check your answers.

listen carefully

2 Look at the table.

1 Fill in what you can.

2 Listen to Marcella and Nigel again and complete the table.

	1 Marcella	2 Nigel
Who did they speak to?		
Where? What about?		
How did they feel about it?		

listening challenge

3 (1.4) Listen to Juliet describing a conversation in a pub with a stranger. Work with a partner.

1 Why was it unusual?

2 Listen again with the tapescript if you need to.

listening booklet *p.2 to p.5 for tapescripts and exercises*

grammar question forms

1 Complete the questions by adding one missing word.

example What⎸Angela do? *does*

1 Who did Marcella talk?
2 Why the doctor become a courier?
3 works in the Accounts Department?
4 How did the man spend in prison?
5 What did the bank robber look?
6 What did he go to prison?

2 Work in A / B pairs.

A read out questions 1 to 3. B answer them.

B read out questions 4 to 6. A answer them.

3 Use the prompts below to write five questions to ask your partner.

1 What / do?
2 What / English for?
3 Who / look like / your family?
4 Where / live exactly?
5 How long / live / present home?
6 Where / go / next holiday?
7 Which countries / like / go to?
8 Who / live with?

4 With your partner, ask and answer the questions you wrote.

go to **language reference** *p.151*

grammar question tags

If you want to check what you think is true, or confirm information, you can use a question tag.

1 Say the examples, with falling intonation on the tags.

examples A Marcella was queueing for tickets, wasn't she? ⌁⟶
B Yes, that's right. ⌁⟶
A Juliet met the man in a pub, didn't she?
B Yes, she did.

2 Complete the questions with the correct tag.

1 The courier's a doctor, _____ ?
2 Juliet was really surprised, _____ ?
3 Nigel works in an office, _____ ?
4 Marcella enjoyed talking to the courier, _____ ?
5 Nigel's going to look for a new job, _____ ?
6 Malcolm and Angela have got engaged, _____ ?

3 With a partner, use the questions in **exercise 2** to make dialogues.

example A The courier's a doctor, isn't he?
B Yes, that's right.

go to **language reference** *p.152*

it's your turn!

1 Think! Choose a topic from **exercise 3** on *p.10* to talk about for one minute. Decide what you're going to say and make notes.

2 Take it in turns to talk about your topics in small groups. Ask each other questions.

reading

first meetings

lead-in

1 Think! The people in the photos have just started talking to each other.

   1 Where are they?

   2 Do you think they know each other?

   3 How do you think their conversations started?

2 Compare your ideas with a partner.

3 Look at the **natural English** box.

   1 Which phrases do you think the people in the photos might have used?

   2 Add two more phrases of your own.

natural English
conversation openers   1.5

Excuse me, is anyone sitting here?
Sorry, have you got the time, please?
I think we've met before, haven't we?
It's really hot, isn't it?
Are you going all the way to San Francisco?

your own ideas

_____

_____

Listen and say the phrases.

4 Think of a possible response for each opener.

example
A Excuse me, is anyone sitting here?
B No, go ahead.

5 Work with a partner.

   1 Practise the openers and responses.

   2 Choose one opener and develop it into a longer conversation.

When **William** met **Jennifer**

I was on the train, on my way home, when I saw Jennifer sitting in the same carriage. My first thought was 'It's *her*'. It was the girl I used to see every day in the library when
05 we were at university. Often I couldn't concentrate on my work when she was sitting so close to me, but in fact, we never spoke once, all the time we were there. And now, eight years later, here she was.

10 So I walked up to her and said, 'We've met before, haven't we? Weren't you at Durham University?' Not a great line, I know, but it **broke the ice**, and we talked for the rest of the journey.

15 We got off the train at the same station, she said goodbye and disappeared. I was **kicking myself** for not getting her telephone number. But then, thank goodness, she came back and said she
20 had to wait on the same platform for her next train. We **carried on** talking, but when her train arrived, I realized I still didn't have her number. This was my last chance. I pushed a pen at her and she
25 **scribbled** her number on a piece of paper just as the train pulled out. I got home and the first thing I said to my flatmate was: 'Do you remember that girl I couldn't stop talking about at university?'
30 and he said, 'Oh, no … yes, of course I remember …' I then talked about her non-stop for an hour. Finally, I phoned her later that evening and we arranged to meet the next day. Six months later we
35 went to Australia and worked together for a year. When we came back, we got married. It's the only thing in my life I've ever felt absolutely certain about. I've never wanted to marry anyone else.

---

read on

1 Read the article and answer the questions with a partner.

  1 Which people on *p.13* is the article about?

  2 What's your reaction to the story?

2 Put sentences a to h in the correct order, according to the text.

  William first saw Jennifer at university …

  a She came back to the same platform.

  b She said goodbye and walked away.

  c He didn't see her again for eight years.

  d He asked her for her phone number.

  e He got angry with himself.

  f They carried on talking.

  g They had their first conversation.

  h He was attracted to her from the start.

  … finally, they went abroad for a year and got married.

3 With a partner, use sentences a to h to tell the story. Add any other details you can remember.

4 Ask and answer these questions.

  1 When was the last time you had a conversation with a stranger?

  2 How long was it, where was it, and what was it about?

grammar present perfect and past simple (1)

1 Look at the speech bubbles on *p.15* and answer these questions.

  1 Underline the verbs in the questions. What tense are they?

  2 Is the man asking about experiences happening before now?

  3 Is he asking <u>when</u> things happened?

  4 Look at the woman's answers. All the *a* answers are in the present perfect. Why?

  5 All the *b* answers are in the past simple. Why?

  6 Circle the words *before*, *ever*, and *just*. Which word means:

    – at any time in your life?

    – at a time before this particular occasion / on a previous occasion?

    – recently / a short time ago?

2 With a partner, ask questions 1 to 3 but give your own answers.

3 Correct any mistakes in these sentences.

  1 I've started learning English last year.

  2 Have you ever forgot to lock your car?

  3 He just has got a new job.

  4 A I'm going to Spain tomorrow.
    B Oh, really? Did you go there before?

  5 I never had a girlfriend, but I'd like one.

  6 Has she seen the film last night?

go to **language reference** *p.152*

1 Complete the sentences about yourself.

think of ...

somewhere interesting you've been

I've _____ .

someone interesting you've met

I've _____ .

something unusual you've **eaten**

I've _____ .

something you've just **done** in your work/studies

I've just _____ .

something you'd **like** to do

I've always wanted _____ .

a **sport** you've never done

I've never _____ .

2 Work in groups of three. Use the prompts in **exercise 1** to talk about yourselves. Ask and answer questions to find out more.

example
A I've been to Iceland.
B Oh, really? When did you go there?
A Oh, it was three years ago, but I'll never forget it ...

📻 extended speaking

Learn these phrases for later
Have you been there before?
I've been there several times.
I've just got married.
Are you going all the way to ...?

wordbooster

jobs

1 Look at the jobs and definitions. Three jobs are in the wrong place. Correct them.

spies	give secret information to other countries
judges	decide what to do with criminals
✈ politicians	look after people in hospital
lawyers	advise and represent people in court
accountants	check company / individuals' finances
✗ **mechanics**	are elected by the people
civil servants	work in government departments
surgeons	operate on people
fashion models	display clothes by wearing them
✗ **nurses**	repair machines and cars
composers	write music
professional sportsmen/women	earn their living from doing a sport

2 Think! Choose two of the above jobs you'd like to do and two you wouldn't like to do. Give two reasons for each choice.

3 Find someone who chose the same jobs as you. Did you have the same reasons?

talking about work

1 Read the questionnaire. Notice the phrases in bold. Mark the stress on the words in *italics*.

Do you know anyone who ...	
1 ... is **training to be** a doctor or a nurse?	
2 ... **works** *freelance*?	
3 ... is **looking for** a job?	
4 ... **works for** a *multinational company*?	
5 ... is *retired*?	
6 ... is *unemployed*?	
7 ... **works in** the *computer industry*?	
8 ... **runs their own** *business*?	
9 ... has recently **given up their job**?	
10 ... has a job which *involves* **a lot of travelling**?	

2 Write the name of someone you know next to each question, if possible.

3 In small groups, say more about the people you thought of in exercise 2.

how to
keep

ask follow-up questions

If you can produce certain questions in English quickly and easily, it will help you to start and keep conversations going.

1 Read conversations 1 and 2 below. Which questions in the box could develop each one? Some questions are possible in both.

> How about you?
> Really? What's it like?
> Have you been there before?
> Is this a business trip, or are you on holiday?
> Whereabouts? /weərə'baʊts/
> How long are you planning to stay?
> Is this the first time you've done ...?
> Is this the first time you've been to ...?

1 A Is anyone sitting here?
   B No, no-one.
   A Thanks. Where are you from?
   B I'm from Japan.

2 A It's really hot, isn't it?
   B Yes, terrible!
   A Are you going all the way to Singapore?
   B Yeah, I am.

2 With a partner, choose one conversation from exercise 1 and develop it using at least three of the questions.

3 Find a pair who chose the other conversation. Act out yours and listen to theirs.

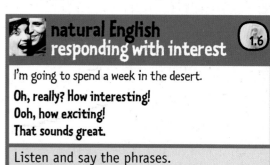

natural English 1.6
responding with interest

I'm going to spend a week in the desert.
Oh, really? How interesting!
Ooh, how exciting!
That sounds great.

Listen and say the phrases.

4 Work in A / B pairs. A turn to *p.144* and B to *p.146*.

a conversation going

party talk

1.  Tune in to the beginning of a conversation between Emma and Clive at a party. Do they sound interested in each other? Why / why not?

2. Listen again and circle the correct answer(s).
   1. Emma is at school / university.
   2. She's studying maths / physics / chemistry.
   3. She's studying / 's hoping to study medicine.
   4. She's thinking of doing the course / some of the course in America.
   5. Clive studied in Australia / the States.

---

natural English
hopes and plans ⟨1.8⟩

I'm going to stay with my uncle.
I'm planning to rent a car.
I'm hoping to get a part-time job.
I'm thinking of going abroad this winter.

When you talk about plans, you don't usually use *will*.

A Are you busy tonight?
B Yes, I'm going to see my sister. NOT ~~I'll see my sister.~~

Listen and say the phrases.

---

go to **language reference** *p.154*

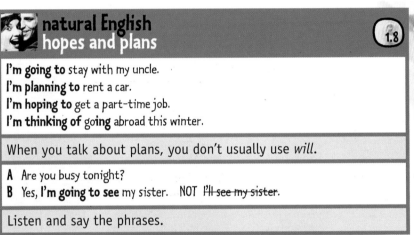

Clive

Emma

it's your turn!

1. **Think!** Use these prompts to write sentences about your own hopes and plans.

travel

your future studies
marriage
your career
your own ideas

2. With a partner, tell each other about one of your hopes or plans. Respond with interest and keep the conversation going.

⟨⟩ extended speaking
Learn these phrases for later
Is this the first time you've been to ...?
What's it like?
Oh really, how interesting!
How long are you planning to stay?

extended speaking

you're going to:

collect ideas
listen to conversations between strangers on a train

create a new identity
prepare and practise being your new character with a partner

role play a conversation
speak to other passengers on a train

write an e-mail
explain what happened in an e-mail to a friend

but first ...
Look back at the **extended speaking** boxes in this unit. You can use this language in the activity.

collect ideas

1   Look at the prompts below. Which details would you tell a stranger on a train? Put a tick ✓ or a cross ✗.

☐ where you come from
☐ if you're married / have children
☐ what you do for a living
☐ how much you earn
☐ why you're travelling
☐ how you're feeling
☐ how old you are
☐ your name

2   Compare ideas with a partner.

3   (1.9) You're going to listen to a conversation between two strangers on a train. In A / B pairs, A read 'the Woman' and B read 'the Man'. Then listen and complete your text.

4   Give your text to your partner. Listen again and check your partner's answers.

the Woman
Her name's ¹_____ and she comes from ²_____. She works as ³_____ and she's travelling on the Orient Express because ⁴_____.

the Man
His name's ¹_____ and he comes from ²_____. He works as ³_____ and he's travelling on the Orient Express because ⁴_____.

create a new identity

5 **Think!** Decide on your new identity and complete a profile of yourself. Use the notes below to help you.

PROFILE

NAME

NATIONALITY

AGE — younger or older than your real age?

MARITAL STATUS — single? married? divorced? widowed? children?

PROFESSION — job? experience? retired? unemployed?

REASONS FOR THE JOURNEY — love? on business? for a holiday? something mysterious?

PREVIOUS TRIPS TO VENICE / ON THE ORIENT EXPRESS — If so, when? Why?

SPECIAL PROBLEM — e.g. you've got flu; the police are following you; you think the train is cold

6 Using your profile, ask and answer questions to practise your new identity with a partner.

 ### natural English
responding with sympathy and understanding

What a pity! What a shame! (when you hear sad or disappointing news)
I am sorry. How terrible! (when you hear more serious or shocking news)

Say the phrases.

 ## role play a conversation

7 In new groups, imagine you are strangers on a train who meet in the buffet car. Find out all you can about each other.

8 Look at each others' profiles. Check for any missing details.

9 At the end of your journey, the police board the train and arrest one member of your group. Decide who and why.

 ## write an e-mail

10 Write an e-mail to a friend, explaining what happened on the train.

---

lost in the desert

he hasn't got any water left his water is finished (picture 2)

camel the animal in picture 3

tie /taɪ/ what the man is holding in picture 4

how to ... react to a joke

That's a good joke.

That's silly.

I don't get it.

That's very funny!

I've heard it before.

do you get it?

with a partner ...

Have you been on any of these holidays? Did you enjoy it?
Why / why not?

a beach holiday	a holiday in the desert /ˈdezət/
skiing holiday	a walking and camping holiday
a sailing holiday	a sightseeing /ˈsaɪtsiːɪŋ/ holiday

Which of the holidays would you definitely not enjoy?

joke time

Look at the pictures. What's happening in each one?
What's going to happen next?

2.1 Listen and react to the joke. Did you get it?
Go to *p.6* of the listening booklet and listen again.

 be / have got sth left

He hasn't got any water **left**. = He had some water, but now he hasn't got any.
I've got two matches **left**. = I had more, but I only have two now.
There's nothing left in the fridge. = There was food, but now there isn't.

Say the phrases. Make sentences about these situations.

1 You had eight oranges; you ate five.
2 There were lots of people; most went home.
3 You had some bread, but you ate it all.

types of journey

Circle the correct word in each sentence.

1 Did you have a good travel/trip to Germany?
2 Do you have an easy journey/trip to work?
3 How long did your flight/fly take?
4 We visited lots of new companies, so it was a successful journey/trip.
5 Japanese tourists often do a European tour/excursion.
6 I try not to voyage/travel during the rush hour if possible.

in unit two ...
tick ✓ when you know this

natural English
be / have got sth *left* ☐
giving opinions, agreeing and disagreeing ☐
talking about priorities ☐
postcard language ☐
offers and requests ☐

grammar
comparatives and modifiers ☐
superlatives ☐
present simple and continuous ☐

vocabulary
types of journey ☐
adjectives describing journeys ☐
everyday problems ☐

wordbooster
hotel rooms ☐
compound nouns ☐

21

listening

travelling can be fun

lead-in

1 Do the questionnaire as a class. Ask questions and give details.

2 Tell the class about one person's answer.

TRAVEL QUESTIONNAIRE

Find someone who ...	name
has an interesting journey to work/school/college	
has several ways of getting to work/school/college	
hates going on long journeys	
would enjoy a trip to Disneyworld©	
travels a lot for work or pleasure	
never travels in the rush hour	
has had a bad experience on a flight	
wants to do a world tour in their lifetime	

vocabulary adjectives describing journeys

1 Mark the stress on the first six adjectives with three or more syllables. Practise saying all the adjectives.

one syllable		
safe	slow	fast
cheap	nice	

two syllables		
noisy	boring	stressful
tiring	quiet	easy
useful	smelly	
useless	bumpy /ˈbʌmpi/	

three or more syllables	
relaxing	(un)comfortable /(ʌn)ˈkʌmftəbl/
dangerous	frustrating /frʌˈstreɪtɪŋ/
exciting	(in)convenient /(ɪn)kənˈviːnɪənt/
(im)practical	luxurious /lʌgˈʒʊərɪəs/
romantic	(un)reliable /(ʌn)rɪˈlaɪəbl/
enjoyable	(in)appropriate /(ɪn)əˈprəʊprɪət/

listen to this

tune in

1   Look at the photos. What are the different forms of transport?

2   You're going to listen to Julia and then Marcella describing trips on unusual forms of transport. Listen to the beginning of both stories.

   1   Where did they go?

   2   What form of transport was it?

listen carefully

3   Listen to the complete stories. Which statements are true of Julia's story, and which of Marcella's story?

   1   There were three people.

   2   There was no noise at all.

   3   The speaker was afraid.

   4   She could see steam.

   5   She enjoyed the whole experience.

   6   She had mixed feelings about the experience.

listening challenge

4   Listen to Juliet, who went on a rickshaw in Cuba.

   1   Tell a partner about Juliet's experience.

   2   Listen again and check with the tapescript if you need to.

5   Have you been on an unusual form of transport? Where, when, and what was it like? Tell a partner.

listening booklet *p.6 and p.7 for tapescripts and exercises*

---

2   Complete each sentence with an adjective from **exercise 1**.

   1   The buses are always late and sometimes don't come at all. They're totally _____ .

   2   Flying first class is so _____ ; champagne, great food, and lots of room.

   3   The trip was very _____ ; the tour guide was excellent, the scenery was beautiful, and I met some great people.

   4   My new office is a long way from the station, which is a bit _____ .

   5   The traffic wasn't moving at all, which was very _____ because the road we wanted was only 100 metres away.

   6   I hate cities; too many people and cars, and so noisy. I find it very _____ .

   7   Flying through bad weather isn't dangerous, but it can be _____ .

   8   The toilets on long-distance coaches can get a bit _____ .

3   In groups, take it in turns to say a sentence about these topics. Use as many adjectives as possible.

   – public transport in your town

   – air travel

   – driving in your town centre

   – intercity travel by train or bus

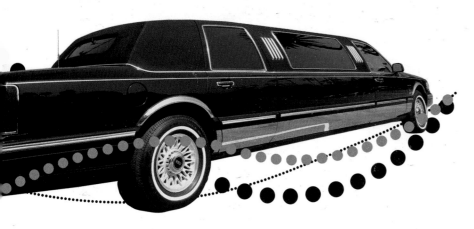

grammar comparatives and modifiers

1 In A / B pairs, A say an adjective from **vocabulary exercise 1** on *p.22* and B say how the comparative is formed.

adjective +*er*   adjective +*r*
adjective –*y* +*ier*   *more / less* + adjective

You can put other words before comparatives to modify the meaning.

2 Write these phrases in the appropriate column.

much cheaper (than)   **a little** cheaper (than)
a bit cheaper (than)   **slightly more** expensive (than)
far more expensive (than)   **a lot** cheaper (than)

a big difference in price	a small difference

3 Choose one phrase from each column which is more informal.

4 Name two examples of the following in your country.

– magazines, e.g. *Elle, National Geographic*

– cars from your country

– forms of transport in your town

– well-known clothes shops

– places to eat in your town

5 Compare the prices of your examples in **exercise 4**.

example   I think *Elle* is a bit more expensive than *National Geographic*.

go to **language reference** *p.154*

it's your turn!

1 **Think!** Decide on the best form of transport for each situation and be prepared to explain your choice.

1	You're going to a wedding in the town centre	by limousine by scooter
2	You're going to ask someone to marry you	in a hot air balloon in a helicopter
3	You're going trekking through the mountains	on a camel on a donkey
4	You're going to have a New Year's Eve party	on a plane on a river boat
5	You're going to rob a bank	on a tandem on a motorbike

giving opinions, agreeing and disagreeing

I think we should take the plane. **Yes, I agree.**
(Personally,) I don't think we should go by train. **No, maybe not.**
I think it would be better to hire a car. **I'm not sure about that.**
Say the phrases and replies.

2 Compare your ideas from **exercise 1** in small groups.

extended speaking

Learn these phrases for later
The centre of town is far more convenient.
It'll be a bit quieter.
I think we should …
I think it would be better to …

wordbooster

hotel rooms

1 **Which items would you expect to find in an average hotel room in your country?**

mirror	lift	table lamp
curtains	coffee table	rugs
sofa	stools	wardrobe
cushions	washbasin	fan
taps	four-poster bed	balcony

2 **Study the photo of the room on *p.26* for one minute. Shut your book and tell a partner everything you can remember about it.**

compound nouns

1 **Match words from left to right to form ten compound nouns.**

snack	pool
swimming	court
beauty	service
tennis	salon
booking	agent
table	conditioning
air	shop
room	tennis
gift	office
travel	bar

2 **The stress is usually on the first part of a compound noun. Say the compounds in exercise 1.**

examples <u>coffee</u> table   <u>bus</u> stop

3 **With a partner, make as many compounds as you can with these four words.**

tennis _____

swimming _____

_____ shop

_____ room

4 **Check your ideas in a dictionary. Which pair has the most correct compounds?**

go to **language reference** *p.156*

reading

what makes a great holiday?

lead-in

1 Ask and answer these questions with a partner.

  1 What's the best holiday you've ever had?

  2 Where did you stay, and who did you go with?

2 **Think!** Decide what makes a good holiday. Tick ✓ the three most important things in the list. Put a cross ✗ for one thing that isn't important. What are your reasons?

luxurious accommodation	great beaches
interesting places to go sightseeing	romance
adventure and excitement	delicious food
good nightlife	good weather
good company (people you like being with)	peace and quiet

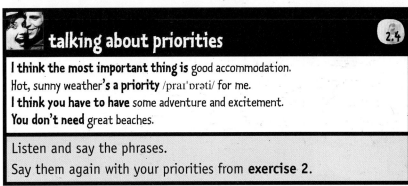

talking about priorities   2.4

I think the most important thing is good accommodation.
Hot, sunny weather**'s a priority** /praɪˈprəti/ for me.
I think you have to have some adventure and excitement.
You don't need great beaches.

Listen and say the phrases.
Say them again with your priorities from **exercise 2.**

3 In small groups, compare your priorities and reasons.

4 Imagine you are going to stay in a luxurious hotel suite. List ten things you would expect to find in your suite.

read on

1 Read the article and complete the glossary. Does the hotel suite have any of the things in your list from **exercise 4**?

2 Read the article again. Write T (true) or F (false).

1 The hotel has 18 rooms.
2 The suite has its own private lift.
3 The four-poster bed has its own television.
4 You can listen to music in every bathroom.
5 You can get on to the balcony from most rooms.
6 There are palm trees in the suite.

grammar superlatives

1 Complete the gaps with the superlative form of the adjective in brackets.

examples

The _funniest_ (funny)

The _most beautiful_ (beautiful)

1 The _____ (interesting)
2 The _____ (good)   } thing about the suite is ...
3 The _____ (bad)
4 The _____ (incredible)
5 The _____ (silly)
6 The _____ (attractive)

2 Tell a partner your opinion of the suite using the phrases in **exercise 1**. Would you like to stay there?

go to **language reference** p.154

THE MOST EXPENSIVE HOTEL SUITE IN THE WORLD $

THE BRIDGE SUITE at the Royal Towers of Atlantis on Paradise Island in the Bahamas has been built with royalty, and the incredibly famous or rich in mind.
05 One night in this luxurious suite of 18 rooms will cost you $20,000. And if you **damage** a piece of furniture it could cost you a lot more, because the cheapest **item** in the suite is a lamp at $6,000.

As you step out of your guarded, private lift, the
10 first thing you see is an Italian gold-leaf mirror that cost $36,000. Your eye may also be attracted to two Picasso plates on the wall, or the two $16,000 silk rugs on the floor.

To your left is a bedroom, a walk-in wardrobe,
15 and one of five showers and four toilets. The suite is suspended 50 metres in the air between two sections of the hotel, and is said to be the only suite in the world that has nothing above or below it.

glossary

damage (v) /'dæmɪdʒ/ break, physically harm
item /'aɪtəm/ single thing/object
_____ (para 5) large fish that can attack people
ego boost something that makes you feel important
_____ (para 6) famous person

No mini-bar here: guests have their own bar
area (including gold-gilt bar stools at $9,000),
and the bar is stocked with the best champagne
and every other drink imaginable. If you don't feel
like pouring your own drinks, you needn't worry –
a barman is available. The 200 square metre
entertainment room, which includes a grand
piano, has a futuristic stereo system, and there
are speakers in every room, including the toilets.
The four-poster bed in the main bedroom has
hand-painted red and gold curtains with its
own video and television system inside.

From every room you can step out onto the 25
metre-long balcony and take in views of the
sea, palm trees, and pools, many of which are
filled with sharks, turtles, and exotic fish.

HOWARD KARAWAN, senior vice-president of sales and
marketing, says of the Bridge Suite,
'There is nothing like it in the
world for the person staying there.
It is a massive **ego boost** just to know that
5,000 other hotel guests are looking up at
your room and wondering who is sleeping
there and if they are a celebrity.'

it's your turn!

1   You're staying in the Bridge Suite. Work with a partner. You're
going to send a postcard to another pair in your class. Discuss what
you're going to write about, using the ideas below or your own.

– the weather or the food

– interesting or funny things about the hotel

– the most incredible or the silliest feature of your suite

– what you're planning to do during the week

ROYAL TOWERS OF ATLANTIS, PARADISE ISLAND

Hi ———— ,

We've been on Paradise Island for
a couple of days now. ————!
We're staying ...

PHOTO: F. ANASTASIA
CONCEPT: B. HENRYROY

032
567

FLOPAS INTERNATIONAL
PRINTED IN THE USA

THE BAHAMAS

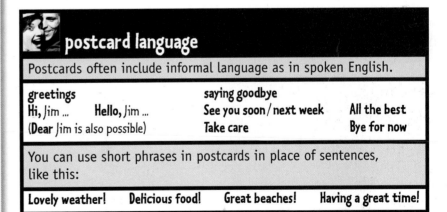

postcard language

Postcards often include informal language as in spoken English.

greetings	saying goodbye	
Hi, Jim ... Hello, Jim ...	See you soon / next week	All the best
(**Dear** Jim is also possible)	Take care	Bye for now

You can use short phrases in postcards in place of sentences,
like this:

| Lovely weather! | Delicious food! | Great beaches! | Having a great time! |

2   Write your card together. Use language from the **natural English** box.

3   Give your postcard to the people you wrote to. What do they
think of it?

extended speaking

Learn these phrases for later

I think the most important thing is ...

Peace and quiet is a priority.

You don't need ...

The best thing about it is ...

how to ...
make a complaint

If you want to make a complaint in English, it's easier if you <u>plan</u> how to explain the problem and its consequences, and ask for action if necessary.

vocabulary everyday problems

1 Look at the problems you might have in a rented holiday villa. With a partner, match the problems 1 to 7 with the pictures, and with consequences a to g.

1 **I'm having problems with** the bathroom taps.

2 The TV **isn't working properly** …

3 The phone's **out of order** …

4 The washing machine's **leaking** …

5 The fan **isn't working** …

6 **I'm having problems** locking the front door.

7 **There's something wrong** with the iron.

a and I need to ring my family.

b They keep dripping and I can't turn them off.

c and the living room is incredibly hot.

d I can't turn the key.

e and we can only get one channel.

f It's just not getting hot enough.

g and there's water all over the floor.

2 (2.5) Listen and check. Say sentences 1 to 7.

test your partner

– *I'm having problems with the bathroom taps.*

– *They keep dripping and I can't turn them off.*

– *That's right.*

3 Think of other problems and complete the sentences.

example My video recorder isn't working, so I can't tape the film this evening.

1 The _____ is leaking and _____
_____ .

2 The _____ isn't working properly, so _____ .

3 I'm having problems with _____ , and _____ .

4 There is something wrong with _____ , and _____ .

grammar present simple and continuous (1)

1 What's the difference in meaning between a and b?

1 a My washing machine's leaking.
  b My washing machine leaks.

2 a I'm having problems with the computer.
  b I have problems with computers.

2 Underline the correct verb form in each sentence.

1 Every time I pick up / 'm picking up the phone, it makes a funny noise.

2 They build / 're building a petrol station next to the hotel; the noise is terrible.

3 Some people sit / are sitting at our table, so we can't have our lunch.

4 The cleaner usually comes / is usually coming in while we're out, but nobody's cleaned the room today.

5 We can't sleep because the guests upstairs have / are having a party.

go to **language reference** *p.155*

get someone to help

1 You're going to listen to two guests staying in holiday villas, who are explaining their problems to the manager. Tune in to the beginning of **conversations 1** and **2**. What problems do they have?

2 Read the conversation summaries.

> ## The manager asks what the problem is and the guest explains politely that her washing machine isn't working; it stops after ten seconds. She's staying at the villa for two weeks. The manager offers to look at it himself the next morning at 9.30. The guest is happy.

> ## The guest explains that there's a problem with the door lock. It took him a long time to get in last night. The key won't go in the lock. Last week he had a problem with the kitchen tap and it's still broken. The manager offers to send someone to look at it later in the day.

3 Listen and correct any factual mistakes in the summaries.

offers and requests

| **I'll get someone to** have a look at it. |
| That's great. |
| **I'll ask the electrician to** come and repair it. |
| Lovely, thank you. |
| **Could you get someone to** have a look at it? |
| Yes, of course. |
| Underline examples in the tapescript on *p.8* of the **listening booklet**. Say the phrases and responses. |

4 Work with a partner.

A You're staying in a holiday villa. Explain one of the problems below, and ask the manager for help if necessary.

B You're the manager. Listen to the problem, ask questions if necessary, and offer to help.

The bathroom floor is dirty.   The air conditioning is very noisy.
The TV isn't working.   You can't open the window.

5 Change roles, and choose a different problem.

 extended speaking
Learn these phrases for later
The ... isn't working.   There's something wrong with ...
I'm having problems with ...   Could you get someone to have a look at it?

extended speaking

a holiday complex

you're going to:

collect ideas
plan your holiday complex: who it's for, where it will be, and what facilities it will have

prepare a presentation
decide exactly how to present your complex to another group

present your ideas
give your presentation and decide which group has designed the best holiday complex

role play
act out a role play at the complex

but first ...
Look back at the **extended speaking** boxes in this unit. You can use this language in the activity.

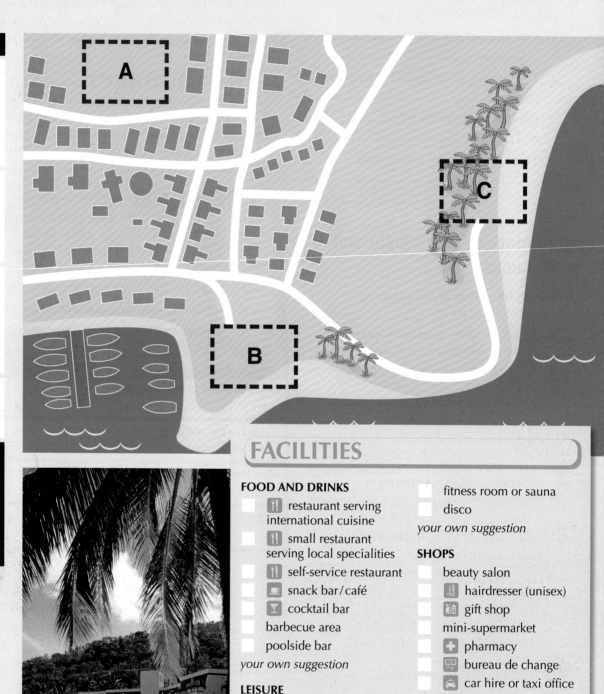

FACILITIES

FOOD AND DRINKS
- restaurant serving international cuisine
- small restaurant serving local specialities
- self-service restaurant
- snack bar / café
- cocktail bar
- barbecue area
- poolside bar

your own suggestion

LEISURE
- swimming pool
- children's paddling pool
- tennis court
- table tennis
- attractive gardens

- fitness room or sauna
- disco

your own suggestion

SHOPS
- beauty salon
- hairdresser (unisex)
- gift shop
- mini-supermarket
- pharmacy
- bureau de change
- car hire or taxi office

your own suggestion

SPECIAL ATTRACTIONS/ SERVICES

1 _____

2 _____

collect ideas

1 Your complex will be in or near a small town on the coast, and will be big enough for 150 people. In groups of three or four, decide on your customer profile.

- ☐ young people aged 18 to 25
- ☐ families with small children
- ☐ retired people / couples aged 55+

2 Look at the map. Decide on the best location (A, B, or C) for your complex and the reasons for your choice.

3 **Think!** Look at the possible facilities for your complex.

1 Tick ✓ three from each section.

2 Invent two special attractions or services.

4 Compare ideas in your group and make your final decisions.

 ## prepare a presentation

5 You're going to present your holiday complex. Read the checklist and prepare as a group.

> **checklist**
> – Remember to include the following information and the reasons behind your decisions.
>   1 the age group   3 the facilities
>   2 the location   4 your two special attractions
> – Divide up your presentation so that each member of your group has a turn.
> – Use notes if you like, but when you give your presentation, don't read your notes aloud. Look at the people you are talking to.
> – Rehearse exactly what you are going to say to give you confidence.
> – Prepare to begin your presentation using a present perfect verb phrase.
>   *examples* We've chosen a holiday complex for …
>   We've decided to have …

 ## present your ideas

6 Work with another group. Take it in turns to give your presentations. When you are listening, think of questions to ask at the end.

7 Decide which group designed the best complex, and why.

 ## role play

8 In A / B pairs, A turn to *p.144* and B to *p.146*. Act out the role play.

9 Swap roles. A turn to *p.146* and B to *p.144*.

---

test yourself!

How well do you think you did the extended speaking? Mark the line.

0 ———————————————— 10

From this unit:

1 write the comparative forms for: *noisy, boring, dangerous, useful.*

2 complete these things you find in a bedroom: wa _____ , cu _____ , la _____ , mi _____ , ru _____ .

3 complete these compound nouns: snack _____ , travel _____ , tennis _____ , coffee _____ , air _____ .

Complete the sentences. The meaning must stay the same.

1 Monaco is far more expensive than Lisbon.
Lisbon is much _____ .

2 I had £50; I spent £40.
I've only got _____ .

3 The phone isn't working.
There's _____ .

4 It would be better to stay here.
We _____ .

Correct the errors.

1 It's a bit more cheaper.

2 The children still play, so we can't leave yet.

3 The more incredible thing about the hotel is the food.

4 It's a long travel to the airport.

Look back at the unit contents on *p.21*. Tick ✓ the language you can use confidently.

life with Agrippine

in groups ...

Do you sing? If so, where and when, and what sort of things? Do you know anyone who sings well?

cartoon time

Read the cartoon. Why does Agrippine say 'Be quiet!' in the first picture, but 'OK, sing!' in the last picture?

Do you think this is a typical brother-sister relationship?

3.1 Listen and follow the cartoon. Then make example sentences with the glossary words.

---

 natural English
me too / me neither   **3.2**

same opinion	A I like this one.	A I don't like this.
	B Yeah, **me too.**	B No, **me neither.**
different opinon	A I like this one.	A I don't like this.
	B **Really? I don't.**	B **Really? I do.**

Listen to the dialogues. Practise with a partner.

Think! Decide on an example of something you like or don't like from these categories. Tell a partner and agree / disagree with their ideas.

| food / drink | a TV programme | a sport / hobby | clothes | weather |

---

glossary

glad happy / pleased
shut up! ◎ be quiet!   *v. rude / uncouth; unacceptable in most circumstances for adults*
sing out of tune sing the wrong musical notes
awful terrible
stink (v) ◎ smell bad
lyrics /ˈlɪrɪks/ words of a song

---

in unit three ...
tick ✓ when you know this

natural English

me too / me neither	☐
on my / your own, by myself / yourself,	☐
alone, lonely	
like, such as, and that sort of thing	☐
imprecise periods of time	☐
fun (n), *funny* (adj)	☐
talking about memories	☐
never used to	☐

grammar

present perfect and past simple (2)	☐
past simple and *used to* + verb	☐

vocabulary

music	☐
stages in your life	☐

wordbooster

likes and dislikes	☐
verb + noun collocation	☐

reading
a perfect day

lead-in

1 Think! Decide on your idea of a perfect day.

1 Where would you go?
2 What would you do?
3 Who would you spend the day with?
4 What would the weather be like?

2 Compare your answers in small groups.

natural English
on my / your own, by myself / yourself, alone, lonely

You can use *on my / your own* more in spoken English and *by myself / yourself* in both written and spoken English. *Alone* is neutral in meaning but *lonely* means 'unhappy to be alone'.

I'd be happy to go to the cinema **on my own / alone**. NOT ~~by my own~~
I'd go for a swim **by myself / alone**.

Say the phrases.

3 Imagine a perfect day spent on your own. Tell a partner three or four things you would be happy to do by yourself.

4 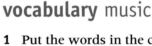 Read the lyrics of *Perfect Day* on **3.3** *p.10* of the **listening booklet**. Listen and correct nine mistakes.

5 Ask and answer with a partner.

1 What do you think of the song?
2 Was Lou Reed's idea of a perfect day similar to yours?

vocabulary music

1 Put the words in the correct column. Say the words and phrases.

lead singer	orchestra /ˈɔːkɪstrə/
songwriter	soloist /ˈsəʊləʊɪst/
composer	keyboard player /ˈkiːbɔːd pleɪə/
solo artist	violinist /vaɪəˈlɪnɪst/
drummer	bass guitarist /beɪs gɪˈtɑːrɪst/
group / band	conductor /kənˈdʌktə/
choir /ˈkwaɪə/	

(handwritten annotations: pianist, fiddle player, percussionist, quartet, band leader (big band))*

rock and pop	classical music and opera

2 Put the stages in the most probable order. Compare with a partner.

- write the lyrics
- record the song
- release the song
- choose a recording artist
- the song becomes a hit
- write the music

3 With a partner, write four questions about music using vocabulary from **exercises 1** and **2**.

examples Who's the lead singer of …?
Which composer wrote …?
Who recorded …?

4 Ask another pair your questions.

read on

SCAN for answers.

1,2 Read the article with the glossary.

2 In the article, find: *1 minute*

1 three ways *Perfect Day* was used after 1972. *trainspotting/BBC ad/charity*

2 one way *Candle in the Wind* was used. *Diana's funeral*

3 one way *Nessun Dorma* was used. *Italian Football World Cup 1990*

3 **Think!** Which songs do you find very memorable or sad? Tell a partner.

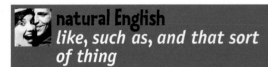

natural English
like, such as, and that sort of thing

I like music **such as** opera, choral music, and classical music.
I really love modern music **like** ☺ house, rap, reggae, and hip hop.

After one or two examples, we can use an expression meaning 'et cetera'.

I'm fond of opera, **and that sort of thing**. ☺
I like jazz, rock, **and that sort of thing**.

Practise saying the sentences. Find other examples in the article.

4 Complete these sentences using suitable phrases from the **natural English** box.

1 I enjoy films _____ .
2 I love sports _____ .
3 I don't like _____ .

5 Compare your ideas with a partner.

lives of the great songs

05 It's difficult to imagine that a song on an album from 1972 could become an enormous hit more than 25 years later. But that is exactly what happened to *Perfect Day* by Lou Reed. First, it appeared in the film *Trainspotting* starring Ewan McGregor and Robert Carlyle, and then the BBC made a new recording of it as an advertisement for themselves. They asked 27 famous artists from around the world to sing or play a line from the 10 song in their own style. The final video included people such as David Bowie, Elton John, Bono, opera singer Lesley Garrett,

Tom Jones, Suzanne Vega, and Lou Reed himself, as well as a symphony orchestra, a gospel choir, and a 15 classical quartet. Lou Reed was **delighted** with the final video: 'I have never been more impressed with a performance of one of my songs.' It was also released for a 20 children's **charity**, and that's when it became a really big hit and earned over £1,000,000.

Another song that raised money for charity was *Candle in the Wind* by Elton John. This song was originally written in 1973 as a tribute to 25 Marilyn Monroe. It describes how she became a Hollywood superstar, but this fame did not make her happy. The press followed her everywhere, making her life difficult, and she was very lonely. After the death of Princess Diana in 1997, Elton John changed the lyrics and sang it at her **funeral**. In the Diana version, he describes her 30 as 'the nation's golden child' who brought happiness to so many people. It became the biggest-selling record of all time.

And it is not only pop music that is used in new ways. The works of classical composers like Beethoven and Vivaldi are often used in films, TV, and advertisements. The Italian opera composer Puccini 35 could never have imagined that his aria *Nessun Dorma* from *Turandot* would become famous all over the world as the **theme tune** for the 1990 football World Cup in Italy.

glossary

Match the words and definitions.

1 **delighted** /dɪˈlaɪtɪd/
2 **charity** /ˈtʃærəti/
3 **funeral** /ˈfjuːnərəl/
4 **theme tune** /ˈθiːm tjuːn/

a song associated with a film, programme, or special event

b ceremony (usually religious) when someone dies

c very happy

d organization which collects money for the poor or sick

listening
what's happened to you?

lead-in

1 **Think!** Write down three sentences about your life. Two must be true, and one false.

examples I've been on television.
I spent six days on my own in the desert last year.
I've broken my arm twice.

2 Work in small groups. Take it in turns to read out your sentences and decide which one is false.

grammar present perfect and past simple (2)

1 Look at the pictures of Paul's musical and artistic history below. Circle the correct verb form in the sentences.

example He (learnt) / has learnt to play the piano when he was a child.

1 He studied / has studied the piano for two years when he was young.
2 He didn't play / hasn't played the piano since he was 12.
3 He took up / has taken up the guitar when he was 15.
4 He studied / has studied at art college for three years.
5 He was / has been out of work for a year.
6 He became / has become a graphic artist 12 years ago.
7 He worked / has worked as a graphic artist since he was 23.
8 He joined / has joined a band in his late twenties.
9 He was / has been in a choir for three years.

2 Use the sentences in **exercise 1** to fill in the gaps in the rules.

past simple
We use the past simple here only to talk about past events or situations. These happened at a specific or known time (e.g. yesterday), or a known period of time (e.g. last summer). The events and situations do not continue up to now.
Sentences: 1, __ , __ , __ , __ , __

present perfect
We use the present perfect here to talk about events and situations which started in the past and continue up to now.
Sentences: __ , __

We use the negative form to talk about something not happening in a period of time from the past to now.
Sentence: __

for / since
Use _____ with the present perfect or the past simple to talk about a period of time.
Use _____ with the present perfect in the main clause to say when something started.

Paul at ... 6   15   17

3 Make five sentences about Paul, using these prompts and the pictures below. Use the past simple or present perfect.

1 join / choir 　　3 have / present job 　　5 be / band
2 play / the guitar 　　4 not be / out of work

example give up / piano 　He gave up the piano when he was 12.

4 Match the phrases and definitions in the **natural English** box.

natural English
imprecise periods of time

1	**for a couple of years**	a	about three or four years
2	**for several years**	b	a relatively long period
3	**for quite a while**	c	a very long time
4	**for ages** /fərˈeɪdʒɪz/	d	about two years

Say the phrases.

5 Which tenses are used in these *How long ...?* questions, and why?

How long did he study the piano?

How long has he sung in a choir?

6 Write four more *How long ...?* questions about Paul.

7 Ask your partner the questions. They must answer using the **natural English** phrases.

go to **language reference** *p.157*

19　　23　　27　　32

listen to this

tune in

1  You're going to listen to Lorelei and Chris talking about their work experience. Listen to the beginning of both conversations.

Chris

Lorelei

1 What do they do?

2 How long have they been in their profession?

3 Can you name one thing each person has done?

listen carefully

2 Listen to the complete conversations and tick ✓ the things they have done.

	acting			writing		radio	commercials	voice-overs
	TV	film	theatre	plays	for TV			
Lorelei						✓		
Chris		✓						

> **natural English**
> ### *fun* (n), *funny* (adj)
>
> *Fun* describes things that are enjoyable, often used with *good* and *great*.
>
> The journey was **great fun**. (= enjoyable) We hired bikes, which was **good fun**.
>
> Don't confuse *fun* (n) with *funny* (adj).
>
> The film is very **funny**. (= it makes you laugh)
> The car's making **a funny noise**. (= a strange noise)
>
> Practise the phrases. Tell a partner:
>
> 1 two things that are great fun. 2 one thing / person you find funny.

listening challenge

3 Listen to Julia talking about acting. Work with a partner.

1 What has she done, and who has she met?

2 Listen again with the tapescript if you need to.

4 Are there any kinds of acting <u>you</u> would like to do?

listening booklet *p.10 to p.13 for tapescripts and exercises*

it's your turn!

1 Think! Choose a famous actor / actress.

1 Approximately how long have they been an actor / actress?

2 What films or TV programmes have they been in, or are they in now?

3 Which is their best film or performance?

4 Have they done other things, for example writing or singing?

5 What do you like about this person?

2 Find a partner. Tell them about your actor / actress, but <u>don't</u> say the name. Can they guess who you are describing?

> 🔊 extended speaking
> **Learn these phrases for later**
> I learnt to play the piano when I was 12.
> I haven't played the guitar for several years.
> How long have you been in your band?
> I sang in a choir for a couple of years.

wordbooster

likes and dislikes

1 Fill the gaps in the words in dialogues 1 to 6.

fantastic	1	**A** I r__lly __ve this painting! **B** Yes, it's gr__t, isn't it?
good	2	**A** I like this one. **B** Yes, it's n__e.
OK	3	**A** I d__'t m__d this. **B** No, it's n__ b__.
not very good	4	**A** I'm not too k__n __ this. **B** No, I'm not m__ about it either.
terrible	5	**A** I don't like this __ a __. **B** Me neither. It's __ful.
	6	**A** I c__'t s__nd this sort of thing. **B** No, me neither. I __te it.

2 Practise the dialogues with a partner until you feel confident.

3 Look at the paintings. Tell three other people what you think of them.

verb + noun collocation

1 Which word in each row of the table doesn't collocate with the verb in the first column?

example	**make**	a mistake	the bed	~~homework~~	money
join	a club	a choir	a university	a group
play	skiing	a computer game	a CD	the drums
give up	the flute	sport	smoking	breathing
practise	your English	sport	the violin	your tennis serve
take up	riding	the guitar	chocolate	acting

2 Ask and answer the questions with a partner and give your reasons.

1 Would you prefer to join a choir or a pop group?
2 Is it easier to give up smoking or chocolate?
3 Which do you think is more fun, playing the drums or the flute?
4 Would you prefer to play computer games or listen to classical music?
5 Is it easier to learn to play the guitar or the violin?
6 Would you prefer to take up golf or baseball?
7 Is it easier to practise your English inside or outside the classroom?

go to **language reference** *p.157*

how to ... talk about your past

There are certain structures and phrases in this lesson which are very useful when you are talking about your past. Using these can make you sound more fluent in English.

do you remember?

1   Ask and answer with a partner.

1   Have you got a good memory?

2   What kinds of things do you find difficult to remember?

> **natural English**
> **talking about memories** 3.6
>
> I can remember _____ -ing _____ very clearly.
> I can just remember _____ -ing _____ .
>   = I can remember, but only a little
> I can't remember _____ -ing _____ at all.
>
> Listen and complete the sentences.
> Practise saying them.

2   Look at the pictures. Can you remember learning to do these things? Tell a partner, using phrases in the **natural English** box.

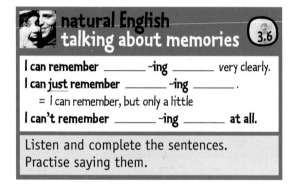

use a computer

swim

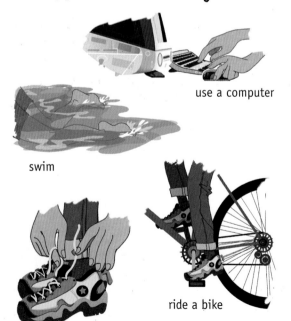

ride a bike

tie your shoelaces

vocabulary stages in your life

1   Look at the table. Tick ✓ the stages you have experienced in your life so far.

Paul McCartney

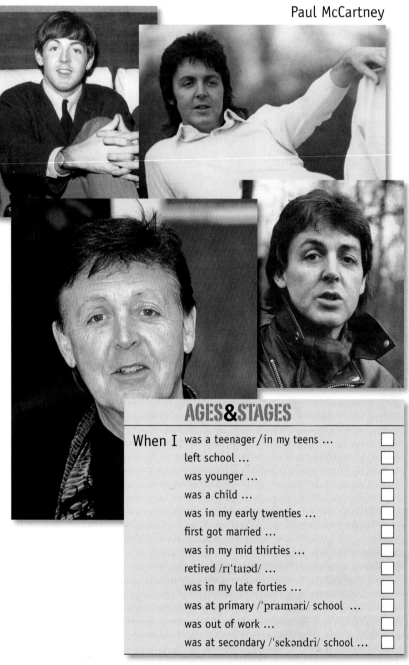

AGES&STAGES

When I		
was a teenager / in my teens ...		☐
left school ...		☐
was younger ...		☐
was a child ...		☐
was in my early twenties ...		☐
first got married ...		☐
was in my mid thirties ...		☐
retired /rɪ'taɪəd/ ...		☐
was in my late forties ...		☐
was at primary /'praɪməri/ school ...		☐
was out of work ...		☐
was at secondary /'sekəndri/ school ...		☐

2   Choose three phrases you ticked. Tell a partner something about this period in your life.

> *example*   When I was at secondary school, I didn't work very hard till I was about 16.

grammar past simple and *used to* + verb

1 **(3.7)** Listen to some people talking about art. Complete the sentences.

1 When I was at primary school, _____ and then draw pictures to go with them.

2 When I was a child, _____ painting lessons at school, but I never liked going round art galleries.

3 When I left school, _____ course at university, but I didn't finish it.

4 I remember when I was younger, _____ all the time. My mum really loved that.

5 When I was in my early twenties, _____ for six months.

2 Check your answers with the tapescript on *p.12* of the **listening booklet.**

3 Answer the questions.

1 Two of the speakers say *used to* in their sentences. What do they mean?

2 Look at the other sentences. When is it possible to say *used to* + verb in place of the past simple?

3 How do you pronounce *used* in sentences 1 and 2? Practise saying the sentences.

---

natural English
never used to

Didn't use to is the negative of *used to*, but in spoken English *never used to* is much more common.

I never used to eat cheese when I was a child.
I love salad now, but **I never used to**.

---

4 Talk about yourself as a child, using *used to* or *never used to*. Use these topics and add two more.

like swimming   drink coffee
go to bed before 8.00   have nightmares
like going to the dentist   cycle to school
your own topics

go to **language reference** *p.158*

---

it's your turn!

1 **Think!** How have your interests changed? Complete the table in note form.

The Arts

interests	when you were younger	nowadays
going to the cinema	*westerns, cartoons*	*not very often, more serious films*
going to the theatre		
drawing and painting		
going to museums or art galleries		
taking / collecting photos		
making things e.g. with wood, materials, etc.		

2 Work in small groups. Tell each other what you used to do / never used to do, and what you do now.

 extended speaking
Learn these phrases for later
When I was a teenager, I used to ...
When I was at secondary school, I started ...
I can clearly remember listening to ...
I never used to ...

you're going to:

collect ideas
read about music in
somebody's life

**prepare for an
interview**
create a
questionnaire and
talk about music in
your life

interview
use your
questionnaire to
interview a partner

write a music profile
use your
questionnaire and
notes to write your
own or your partner's
music profile

but first ...
Look back at the
extended speaking
boxes in this unit.
You can use this
language in the
activity.

 collect ideas

1 Read about music in Maria's life.

  1   Which periods of Maria's life are described in each paragraph?

  2   How has her taste in music changed?

LIFE

MARIAONMUSIC

My earliest memory of music is the songs my mother used to sing to me when I was about three or four. We used to have
05 music lessons at school too; when we were very young, we had singing lessons but we also played musical instruments like the drums while the
10 teacher played the piano. My mother wanted me to take up the violin, but I didn't like it at all, and I gave it up after a year. **Then when I was 10**, I
15 bought my first record with some birthday money. I think it was a record by *The Police* – before Sting became a solo artist.

'MUSIC IS AN IMPORTANT PART OF MY LIFE'

20 **As I got older**, my musical taste changed. When I was a teenager, we used to go to clubs and pop concerts to listen to groups playing
25 live, mostly rock and pop and that sort of thing. **At the time**, I didn't like classical music at all; **later**, when I went to university,
30 I really got into classical music and started going to concerts. I was particularly keen on opera.

Nowadays, I listen to all
35 sorts of music, but I'm not too keen on loud rock music. On the whole, I prefer classical music and opera, but I still listen to
40 pop music in my car. I haven't been to any concerts for ages, but I've always got a CD on at home. Music is an important part of my
45 life.

'I PREFER CLASSICAL MUSIC AND OPERA, BUT I STILL LISTEN TO POP MUSIC IN MY CAR'

prepare for an interview

2 With a partner, use the prompts and your own ideas to add five questions to the questionnaire.

first record / CD?   musical tastes change?   dislikes?

concerts / clubs?   favourite groups, singers, etc.?   kinds of music?

your own ideas

♪ THE MUSIC QUESTIONNAIRE ♪

1 What are your earliest memories of music?

2 Do / did you have music lessons at school? If so, what were they like?

3 Are you learning / did you learn to play a musical instrument? If so, tell me more!

4 _____ ?

5 _____ ?

6 _____ ?

7 _____ ?

8 _____ ?

3 Think! What answers would <u>you</u> give to the questions? Be ready to say as much as possible. Don't give one word answers.

 interview

4 Read the checklist and then interview a partner.

5 Find a new partner and interview each other.

6 When you've finished, tell the class one interesting thing about music in your partner's life.

 write a music profile

7 Look at the six phrases in **bold** in Maria's profile. They clarify the sequence of events. Use them to structure your profile.

8 Do either a or b. Start writing now, and finish at home.

a   write your own music profile

b   write your partner's music profile, using your notes

9 Show your profile to your partner and ask them to check it. Make any necessary changes.

From this unit, write down:

1   three ways of describing people who perform music together, e.g. *a group*.

2   three nouns which can follow each of these verbs *join, play, take up, practise*.

3   five stages in somebody's life, e.g. *when they were a teenager*.

Complete the sentences. The meaning must stay the same.

1   I hate this record.
I can't _____ .

2   I don't like opera very much.
I'm not too _____ .

3   It's two years since I saw him.
I haven't _____ .

4   I was about 24 or 25 at the time.
I was in _____ .

Correct the errors.

1   He did his homework by his own.

2   She usually play the guitar when she was a child.

3   **A**   How long did you study English?
B   Since September.

4   I can just remember learn to tie my shoelaces.

Look back at the unit contents on *p.33*. Tick ✓ the language you can use confidently.

the kangaroo

how to ... react to a joke

That's quite funny.

That's a nice joke.

That's a terrible joke.

That's an old one.

I don't get it.

do you get it?

with a partner ...

Describe a park that you know well. Do you like going there? Why / why not? What different things do people do there?

joke time

Look at the pictures. What's happening in each one? What's going to happen next?

 4.1 Listen and react to the joke. Did you get it?
Go to *p.14* of the listening booklet and listen again.

4.2

expressing a preference

Would rather is very common in spoken English. It means *would prefer to*.

A Would he like to go to the zoo?	**A** Shall I get her a present?
B No, **he'd prefer to** go to the cinema.	**B** I think **she'd rather** have money.

Listen and practise the dialogues with a partner.
Answer these questions.

Do you want some coffee?	Shall we stay here?
Shall we watch the film now?	How about Peru for our next holiday?

---

go to **language reference** *p.158*

facial actions

Match the words with the pictures. Which word was in the joke?

grin (at sb)	laugh (at sb / sth)	cry
yawn /jɔːn/	whistle /'wɪsl/	wink (at sb)

test your partner
– (do the action e.g. wink)
– You're winking at me!
– That's right.

45

reading
difficult choices

lead-in

1 Fill in the gaps with the correct form of *choice* (n) /tʃɔɪs/ or *choose* (v) /tʃuːz/.

  1 When you eat out, which course do you _____ first?

  2 Have you ever _____ something from a menu without knowing what it was?

  3 Who _____ the last restaurant you went to?

  4 Do you have a wide _____ of restaurants where you live?

2 With a partner, ask and answer the questions.

vocabulary food and drink

1 Label the pictures with words from the list.

  1 well done / rare /reə/ steak

  2 still / sparkling water

  3 shrimps / prawns /prɔːnz/

  4 sugar / sweetener /ˈswiːtnə/

  5 green salad / mixed salad

  6 French fries /frentʃ ˈfraɪz/ / a baked potato

  7 lettuce /ˈletɪs/ / cabbage /ˈkæbɪdʒ/

  8 melon / watermelon

2 Explain the difference between the pairs of words in **exercise 1**.

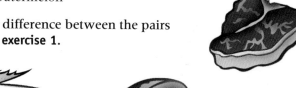

test your partner

– *(point at a picture)*

– *That's a watermelon.*

– *That's right.*

read on

1 British journalist Jonathan Glancey describes what happened to him in the United States. In two groups, A and B, read your texts.

2 With a partner who read the same text, answer the questions.

  1 Who is Jonathan Glancey talking to?

  2 What happens when he tries to order something?

  3 How does he feel: happy? relaxed? impatient?

3 Read your text again. Try to remember:

  1 what Jonathan Glancey wanted.

  2 at least three choices they offered him.

  3 what he chose.

4 In A / B pairs, compare the details you remembered. How would you feel in that situation?

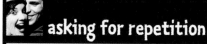

asking for repetition `4.3`

If you don't hear, or aren't clear about what someone said, use these phrases:

Pardon?
Sorry, I didn't quite catch that.
Sorry?
Sorry, I missed that.

Which of these phrases are in the texts? Listen and say the phrases.

Ask / tell your partner something in a very quiet voice. They reply using the phrases.

A
All I want is a burger!

SITUATION ONE: 12.30 p.m.

I walked into a roadside diner in New Jersey, fifty miles from New York City. It was cold and I was very hungry.
'Hi!' said the waitress. 'I'm Jo. Would you like a smoking or no smoking seat?'
05 'Erm, no smoking,' I replied.
'Window seat or inside?'
'Pardon?'
'Window seat or inside?'
'Uh, window.'
10 I quickly looked through a menu the size of an encyclopaedia and chose a cheeseburger.
'Fine. How would you like your burger? Well done, medium, or rare?'
'Medium.'
15 'Would you like it in a sesame **bun** or low-calorie style?'
'I'd rather have a bun.'
'You can have that with French fries or baked potato.'
'All right, french fries.'
'OK, today's side salads are green, mixed, or tomato and
20 onion.'
'Green.'
'Would you like **vinaigrette**, blue cheese, or mayonnaise on that?'
'Vinaigrette.'
25 'OK, I guess you're all set now. Thank you.'
'Oh, I'd like a coffee, too.'
'Fine. We have regular, regular **decaf**, espresso, espresso decaf, capuccino and decaf capuccino,' says Jo. I decide, in the end, to forget the coffee and also avoid a second
30 course. I am really beginning to feel the terrible responsibility of all this decision-making.

B
All I want is a cup of tea!

SITUATION TWO: 6.00 p.m.

I'm lying in my hotel in bed with flu. I am not having a nice day. I **flick through** all 33 channels on the TV, all 33 choices of complete rubbish except for *Bugs Bunny*. I switch off the TV and call room service for a cup of tea.

05 'Is that a regular or a large pot, sir?'
'Regular.'
'Herbal, Earl Grey, or English Breakfast?'
'I'd prefer English Breakfast.'
'Milk or lemon?'
10 'Milk.'
'We have a choice of white sugar, organic sugar, or low-calorie sweetener.'
'Organic sugar?' I ask.
'You want organic sugar?'
15 'No.'
'OK, no sugar.'
By this stage, I was getting a little bit angry.
'Listen,' I said, 'do what you like with the sugar, but just bring me a cup of tea.'
20 'I'm sorry, sir, I didn't quite **catch** the last part of your request.'
'Forget it.'
'You don't want the tea?' he asked.
Actually, I would really like a dry martini, but I'm too
25 frightened to negotiate my way through the range of options available in such an order: gin or vodka, straight or on the rocks, olive or twist of lemon, decaf or …

it's your turn!

1 With a partner, prepare a conversation with a waiter in a café like the ones in texts A and B. Choose two items from the box. Think of three questions the waiter can ask about each item.

a sandwich
a salad
a beer / glass of wine
a coffee
a pizza

2 Take turns to be the waiter. Practise your conversations together.

3 Act out your conversation to another pair.

🎧 extended speaking
Learn these phrases for later
What was your first choice?
I wouldn't choose prawns.
Sorry? I missed that.
What's the difference between ... and ...?

wordbooster

phrases expressing your opinion

1 With a partner, decide whether the phrases have a positive or negative meaning. Say the phrases.

It's a bit boring.	It's intriguing. /ɪnˈtriːgɪŋ/
It's quite interesting. /ˈɪntrəstɪŋ/	It doesn't interest me.
It's very dull. /dʌl/	It's great fun.
It's a waste of time.	I get fed up with it. ☺
It's absolutely fascinating. /ˈfæsɪneɪtɪŋ/	It doesn't appeal /əˈpiːl/ to me.

2 Use the phrases in exercise 1 to tell your partner your feelings about the activities below.

example   A   Surfing the Internet is great fun. I love doing it.
            B   Hmm. It doesn't appeal to me.

surfing the Internet	playing chess	looking after little children
learning how to dive	driving fast	learning a foreign language

3 Add two more activities. How does your partner feel about them?

synonyms

Complete the dialogues with a synonym of the word in bold.

topic	extracts	talk	examine	chance	views /vjuːz/

1 A Would you like another **opportunity** to answer the question?
  B Yes, give me a _____ to try again.

2 A We should **look at** the problems quite carefully.
  B Yes, we need to _____ them in more detail.

3 A She's got some interesting **opinions** about modern art.
  B Yes, I always listen to her _____ .

4 A Did you enjoy the video **clips** she showed us?
  B Yes, the _____ from her latest film were brilliant.

5 A Shall we go to the **lecture** /ˈlektʃə/ at the art gallery this evening?
  B Oh, yes, the woman giving the _____ is brilliant.

6 A I'm afraid the **subject** /ˈsʌbdʒɪkt/ doesn't really appeal to me.
  B Really? I think it's quite an interesting _____ , actually.

test your partner

– What's another word for 'opportunity'?

– Chance.

– That's right.

vocabulary TV programmes

1 Name one TV programme you really like, and one you really don't like and say why.

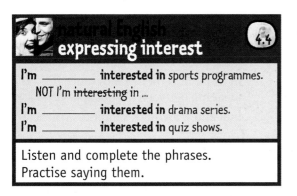

natural English (4.4)

expressing interest

I'm _____ **interested in** sports programmes.
NOT I'm ~~interesting in~~ ...
I'm _____ **interested in** drama series.
I'm _____ **interested in** quiz shows.

Listen and complete the phrases.
Practise saying them.

2 **Think!** Which of these TV programme types do you watch most? Which do you never watch? Can you name an example of each type from your country?

documentaries /ˌdɒkjʊˈmentriːz/
quiz shows /ˈkwɪz ʃəʊz/
comedies (e.g. *Friends*)
sports programmes
news and current affairs /ˌkʌrənt əˈfeəz/
drama series (e.g. *ER*)
chat shows
soap operas /ˈsəʊp ɒprəz/

3 Compare your answers in small groups.

4 Match the subjects of the TV documentaries to the pictures.

1 Hypnosis – does it really work?
2 Choosing your next car
3 Training to be an Olympic athlete
4 Getting started as a fashion model
5 Animal psychologists – what can they do for your pet?
6 How to survive alone in the Amazon rainforest

natural English

saying how much you know

I know (quite) a lot about hypnosis.
I know a bit about animal psychology.
I don't know very much about cars.
I don't know anything about being a fashion model.

Say the phrases.

5 How much do you know about the subjects of the programmes in **exercise 4**? Tell a partner.

example **A** I know quite a lot about hypnosis. How about you?
B I don't know anything about it.

listen to this

tune in

1 You're going to listen to a group of TV executives, who are looking at ideas for the TV documentaries in **vocabulary exercise 4**. They have to decide which programmes to make.

Which programmes do you think would appeal to:

men? young people? women? a family?

2 Listen to Mike. Which programmes does he like and why? Complete his section of the table below.

	Mike	Eric	Mary
programme 1			
reason(s)	it affects _____	a young women would like it because _____ b men would like it because ____ _____	it could help people to _____ _____
programme 2			
reason(s)	a it would appeal to _____ b _____ _____	interesting; beautiful pictures;	[no reason given]

listen carefully

3 Listen to Eric and Mary. Complete the rest of the table.

listening challenge

4 Listen to the rest of the conversation. Which programmes do they decide on? Listen again with the tapescript if you need to.

listening booklet *p.14 to p.17 for tapescripts and exercises*

grammar modal verbs *would, could / might*

1 Look at sentences a to f. Answer the questions below.

a I think it <u>would</u> appeal to all age groups.

b I think it <u>might</u> appeal to all age groups.

c I think this one <u>could</u> be interesting.

d I think it <u>might</u> be interesting.

e This <u>could</u> / <u>might</u> be very interesting.

f This <u>can</u> be very interesting.

1 In a and b, what is the difference in meaning between *would* and *might*?

2 In c and d, is there a difference in meaning between *could* and *might*?

3 In e and f, are both sentences correct?

go to **language reference** *p.159*

2 Work in small groups. Take it in turns to comment on the six programmes using *would* and *could / might*. Give your reasons.

3 **Think!** Decide on three changes you'd like to make to TV programming in your country.

examples

I'd have more programmes about music.

I'd have a special channel for children's programmes.

I wouldn't have so many soap operas.

4 Tell each other in small groups. Do you have the same ideas?

🎧 extended speaking

Learn these phrases for later

I think that might be interesting.

I'd be interested in ...

I don't know much about ...

That could be really interesting.

how to ... make a phone call

answer the phone

1 Correct four mistakes in these telephone dialogues.

1   A   Hello?
      B   Oh, hello, could I speak to David Stone, please?
      A   Yes, I'm speaking.
      B   Oh, good morning. Here is Angela Green and …

2   A   Hello?
      B   Oh, oh, good afternoon. Is that Mrs Carter?
      A   Yes, I am.
      B   Oh, hello. My name's Chris Jackson and …

3   A   Hello?
      B   Oh, hi, Jim, I'm Carrie.
      A   Oh, hi, Carrie. How are you?

2 **(4.7)** Listen and check your answers. Practise the dialogues with a partner.

---

phone greetings

		more informal
identifying the listener	**Is that** Bruno Zola?	**Is that** Bruno?
	Could I speak to Bruno Zola, **please?**	~~Are you Bruno?~~
		Is that you, Bruno?
saying who you are	**(Yes,) speaking.**	**Yes** (it is).
introducing yourself	**My name's** Elena Ponti.	**It's** Elena. ~~I'm Elena.~~
		This is Elena. ~~Here is Elena.~~

How do you say these phrases in your language?

---

give the reason for your call

1 Two students of English are inviting a guest speaker to give a talk at their school. They've never spoken to the person before. Read how they introduce themselves. Which introduction is better, and why?

1   … Oh, hello Mr Peterson. We'd like you to give a talk on American cinema. The students in my school are very interested in this subject.

2   … Oh, hello Mr Peterson. My name's Rosa López. I'm a Spanish student studying English at Oxford College, and I'm ringing to invite you to give a talk at our school in April.

2 You're going to phone and invite Mr Peterson to give a talk. Write your introduction and invitation, using the better model. Then memorize it.

3 Practise the beginning of the phone conversation, including the greetings, with a partner.

invite and make arrangements

1 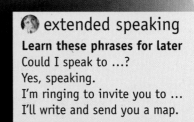 **(4.8)** You're going to listen to Chris Jackson, phoning Anne Carter to invite her to give a talk at a management conference. Tune in to **part 1** of the conversation. What does he want her to talk about?

2 Read the e-mail. Listen to **parts 1** and **2**, and complete it.

From:	**Chris Jackson <cjackson@network.com>**
Date:	Wed 16 March, 10.36 am
To:	Anne Carter
Subject:	**re:** arrangements for talk

Dear Mrs Carter,

I m very pleased that you ll be able to come to our conference and give your talk on different 1 _____ techniques. As I mentioned, the conference will be from 1 to 3 June, and your talk will be on 2 _____ June, from 3 _____ to 4 _____ . The talk should last about 5 _____ , with the rest of the time for questions from the audience of about 6 _____ managers.

We are holding the conference at the 7 _____ _____ , near Cardiff, and we agreed a fee of 8 _____ plus expenses.

You ll find the directions in the attached file. Do give me a ring if you have any questions.

With best wishes, Chris Jackson

grammar uses of *will*

We can use *will* (*'ll*) when we promise, offer, or agree to do something at the moment of speaking.

1 Listen to **part 2** again. Tick ✓ the phrases you hear.

☐ I'll contact you again soon.

☐ I'll give you my e-mail address.

☐ I'll ring you before the talk.

☐ I'll write and send you a map.

☐ I'll get an e-mail off to you.

2 Write two possible offers or promises for statements 1 to 4.

example
Maria wants to leave now.
- OK, I'll ring for a taxi.
- That's all right, I'll give her a lift.

1 I don't know how to get to the hotel.
2 I can't read your writing in this note.
3 My computer's not working.
4 I don't understand this – it's in French.

3 Practise the dialogues with a partner.

go to **language reference** *p.159*

🔘 **extended speaking**

Learn these phrases for later
Could I speak to ...?
Yes, speaking.
I'm ringing to invite you to ...
I'll write and send you a map.

extended speaking
a weekend English course

you're going to:

collect ideas
read information about six possible talks

choose your speakers
decide which two speakers you want to invite

decide on a new talk
agree on a topic and summarize the talk

role play
telephone one of the speakers you chose

but first ...
Look back at the **extended speaking** boxes in this unit. You can use this language in the activity.

collect ideas

1 Look at the weekend programme. Which parts would you enjoy most?

ENGLISH
Weekend Program...

	FRIDAY	SATURDAY	SUNDAY
MORNING		9.30 – 12.30 **English classes** 12.45 – 2.00 **Lunch**	9.30 – 12.30 **English classes** 12.45 – 2.00 **Lunch**
AFTERNOON	3.00 **Arrival; greetings** 3.30 – 6.00 **English classes**	2.00 – 3.15 **Talk 1** 3.30 **Free time**	2.00 – 3.15 **Talk 2** 3.30 **Free time**
EVENING	7.00 **Dinner** 9.00 **Film**	7.00 **Dinner and disco**	7.00 **Farewell party**

2 **Think!** Read the description of a talk about rock and pop music. Would you be interested in this talk? Why / why not? Do you agree with the students' comments below?

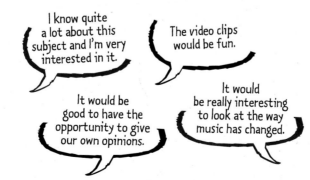

I know quite a lot about this subject and I'm very interested in it.

The video clips would be fun.

It would be good to have the opportunity to give our own opinions.

It would be really interesting to look at the way music has changed.

ROCK AND POP MUSIC

Sunday 2.00pm – 3.15pm
The Souch Lecture Gallery

Music journalist, **Anna Sinclair**, looks at the way rock and pop music have developed over the last thirty years. Some of her views on this subject may surprise you! The lecture is illustrated with music and video clips, and you will have the chance to listen to interviews she has recorded with various groups and solo artists.

3 Compare your ideas with a partner.

choose your speakers

4 **Think!** Read the information about six possible speakers.
For each talk, consider:

- why the subject does or doesn't appeal to you.
- what you specially like or don't like about this particular
  talk (e.g. the use of video, the chance to give your views).

WEEKEND COURSE
TALKS

CAN WE STOP CRIME RISING?

Steve Daly knows a lot about crime after 22 years in prison
for robbery and other crimes. Now a reformed man, Steve will
describe what prison is like and show video clips of prison life.
He will also give his views on helping the younger generation
of criminals, both in prison and when they come out of prison.

AMERICAN CINEMA: IS IT STILL THE BEST?

For years Hollywood and American money dominated world
cinema. But do we still need big budgets and famous stars to
make great films? Young Danish film maker **Jan Peterson**
believes not, and his talk will be illustrated with clips from a
number of recent low-budget European and South American
films.

NEWSPAPERS AROUND THE WORLD

American journalist **Matt de Longi** has worked in
many different countries. He will examine the
power of the press around the world and how it
influences public opinion. He will also show some
of the differences between newspapers in different
countries, and talk about what it is like to be a
journalist.

IS FASHION IMPORTANT?

Every year new fashions appear from Milan or
Paris, but do ordinary people ever wear these
clothes? Designer **Celia Browne** will explain how
designers like Giorgio Armani, Issy Miyake, and
Alexander McQueen influence high street fashion,
and why fashion is important. She will also bring
some clothes for you to try on.

5 In small groups:

1 exchange your opinions about each subject.

2 talk about what the rest of the class might enjoy.

3 decide which two speakers you're going to invite, and why.

6 Tell the rest of the class what you've decided and why.

language reminder introducing opinions

Personally, I think the talk about newspapers
would be ...

~~For me~~ the talk about newspapers would be ...

BRITISH FOOD

You all think it's terrible, don't you? Well, you're wrong! There has been a revolution in British cuisine, and top chef, **Jamie Oliver**, tells you why. Jamie is a very amusing speaker and will bring along some exciting new dishes he has prepared, which you will have a chance to taste and talk about.

MONARCHY OR REPUBLIC?

Historian **Jane Pimlott** believes in the monarchy; journalist **Bob Dwyer** thinks that no country in the 21st century should still have one. They will present their arguments and talk about monarchies and republics around the world. You will have a chance to give your views. At the end there will be a vote.

 ### decide on a new talk

7 Other people attending the course have now said they don't want a film on Friday evening, and would rather have another talk. In your groups, read the checklist and invent a new talk.

> **checklist**
> – Choose a talk you would all be interested in (not the topics above).
> – Think how you can make the talk really interesting, e.g. using video, demonstration, discussion, etc.
> – Give the talk a good title.

8 Write a short paragraph similar to the ones above to describe your talk.

9 Pass your descriptions to other groups to read. Which talks do they like most?

 ### role play

10 In A / B pairs, A turn to *p.144*, and B to *p.148*.

How well do you think you did the extended speaking? Mark the line.

0 _____ 10

From this unit, write down:

1 five types of TV programme, e.g. *sports programmes*.

2 these food items:
   still or _____ water
   green or _____ salad
   well done or _____ steak
   sugar or _____
   baked potato or French _____

3 a synonym for each word: *dull, lecture, opinions, topic, Pardon?*

Complete the sentences. The meaning must stay the same.

1 I'd prefer to go out tonight.
   I'd rather _____ .

2 Sorry, I missed that.
   Sorry, I didn't _____ .

3 I don't find it very interesting.
   It doesn't _____ .

4 It's really enjoyable.
   It's great _____ .

Correct the errors.

1 On the phone:
   A Hello, are you Claudio?
   B Yes, I am.

2 I'm not very interesting in music.

3 A There's someone at the front door.
   B OK, I go.

4 I'm sure that programme might be fascinating.

Look back at the unit contents on *p.45*. Tick ✓ the language you can use confidently.

presents

life with Agrippine

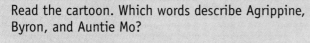

in groups ...

Describe a present you received recently.

What kind of presents do you most/least like to receive? Why?

clothes	CDs	shower/bath products
money	books	perfume/aftershave
chocolates	flowers	*your own ideas*

cartoon time

Read the cartoon. Which words describe Agrippine, Byron, and Auntie Mo?

 well-behaved generous polite kind badly-behaved rude

What would you buy with £50?

5.1 Listen and follow the cartoon. Then test your partner on the glossary words.

natural English
thanking and replying

Thanks (**a lot/very much**).	No problem. ☺
Thank you (**very much indeed**). (more formal)	That's OK.
That was/'s very good/kind of you.	Don't mention it.

How would you thank and reply in these situations?

a stranger gives you directions	a friend gives you a small present
your friend pays for your dinner	a neighbour drives you to the station

glossary

well-behaved /bɪˈheɪvd/ acting politely or correctly (opp **badly-behaved**)

thrilled /θrɪld/ very happy

quid ☺ pound(s) sterling

a little something a small present

mean (adj) not wanting to give money, etc. to others (opp **generous**)

£50 = approx €80 or US$72

 **reading**

lead-in

1 Which do you think is the worst problem, and why? Tell a partner.

- you have to give up smoking
- you have financial problems
- you can't get to sleep at night

natural English | **suggestions and responses** | 5.2

Why don't you try giving up with a friend?
Yes, (that's a) good idea.

Have you thought about hypnosis?
Hmm, I'm not sure about that.

You could avoid places where people smoke.
Yeah, that sounds sensible. /ˈsensəbl/

Listen and say these suggestions and responses with a partner.

Listen and practise again without the book.

2 **Think!** In A / B pairs:

A you can't get to sleep at night.

B you haven't got enough money to buy a computer.

Decide on three suggestions to make to your partner.

3 Make your suggestions and respond to your partner's ideas.

read on

1 Read the article with the glossary.

2 Match these headings to situations 1 to 3.

Please **save** our marriage!

Red faces in public

Sleeping Beauty

best behaviour
by Mary Killen

1

Q During the school holidays my teenage son spends most of his mornings asleep in bed. I think he's <u>unbelievably lazy</u>, but he says it's based on an American theory that people should wake up when their own body clock tells them to, and should not be woken up artificially by alarm clocks or people shouting at them. He <u>reacts angrily</u> if anyone goes near his bedroom. **What can I do?**

A You could buy a cassette of birdsong, and <u>play it loudly</u> outside your son's window when you feel he has had enough sleep. Even if he is aware of the reason why he has woken up, he cannot argue that birdsong is an <u>artificial way</u> to be woken up.

Fill in the gaps and test your partner.

glossary		
can't afford	don't have enough _____	
chauffeur /ˈʃəʊfə/	person who is paid to drive you	
dual /ˈdjuːəl/ **control car**	a driving school car which has controls for both instructor and _____	
solve a problem	find the _____ to a problem	
stare (v) /steə/	_____ at sb/sth for a long time	
upset (adj) /ʌpˈset/	angry and/or unhappy	

Q My wife and I have a terrible time in the car. When I am driving, she is incredibly unpleasant and we have awful arguments about the best route to take. When she is at the wheel, she drives fast and dangerously and it is extremely uncomfortable. We **can't afford** a **chauffeur** or to travel in two separate cars. **What can we do about this?**

A Why don't you go to your local driving school and find out if they have any **dual control cars** which they are prepared to sell you? This could **solve your problem**.

Q My father, aged 65, used to be in the army. He's a lovely man and extremely kind in every way, but when we are out in public together, I always feel embarrassed because he speaks so loudly all the time and everyone **stares** at us. **How can I stop him shouting without hurting his feelings?**

A Why not tell him that you had a terrible experience recently in a restaurant? The couple at the next table were very badly-behaved and shouted at each other throughout the meal. Everyone was clearly **upset** by this. If your father doesn't get the message, you could tell him you've got a headache whenever you go out together.

3 Think! What's your opinion?

1 Do you think the answers in the text are intended to be serious or funny?

2 Which problem has the best solution?

3 Do you think the solutions will work?

4 Can you think of a better solution for one of the problems?

5 Do you know anyone who behaves like the people in the text?

4 Compare your ideas with a partner.

natural English
intensifying adverbs

These adverbs are very common in spoken and informal written English.

It's **extremely** /ɪkˈstriːmli/ uncomfortable.
   (= very, very uncomfortable)
He's **unbelievably** lazy. (= very, very lazy)
She's got an **incredibly** /ɪnˈkredəbli/ good memory.
   (= very, very good)

Listen and mark the stress on the words in **bold.** Say the phrases.

5 Tell your partner three things about yourself and people in your family using the adverbs in the **natural English** box.

grammar adjectives and adverbs

1 Read the rules. Fill in the gaps with the words *adjectives* or *adverbs*.

adjectives and adverbs

1 You can use _____ to modify nouns, e.g. a *casual* shirt, a *big* house.

2 You can use _____ to modify verbs, e.g. he walked *casually*, listen *carefully*, he speaks *fast* (*fast* can be an adjective or adverb).

3 You can modify <u>certain</u> verbs (e.g. *be, seem, look, sound, feel, become, get*) with _____ , e.g. that looks *interesting*, he seemed *angry*.

4 You can use _____ to modify past participles, e.g. *well* made, *badly* written.

5 You can use _____ before certain _____ , e.g. *terribly* cold, *incredibly stupid*.

2 In A / B pairs, A read out an underlined phrase in the article in **read on**, and B match it with a rule in the box. Swap roles after five phrases.

example 'unbelievably lazy' = rule 5

go to **language reference** *p.160*

3 Choose the correct form in the questions below.

1 Do you play loud / loudly music at home?

2 Do you get angry / angrily if someone wakes you up suddenly?

3 Are you ususally smart / smartly or casual / casually dressed?

4 If you drive, do you drive fast / fastly?

5 When you write things down, do you do it careful / carefully?

6 Do you find English pronunciation incredible / incredibly difficult?

7 Do you look good / well in black?

8 Do you speak your own language slow / slowly?

4 With a partner, ask and answer questions 1 to 8.

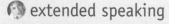 **extended speaking**

Learn these phrases for later

... is extremely unusual in my country.

It's unbelievably expensive.

You don't often hear loud music.

It's important to dress well.

Agne

listening

getting

lead-in

1 Work with a partner.

1 When did you last go to a restaurant?

2 What did you eat?

3 Who did you go with?

4 What did you wear?

dressed up

2 You're meeting someone for dinner at a restaurant this evening, and you're thinking about what to wear. Match phrases 1 to 6 with a to f in the **natural English** box.

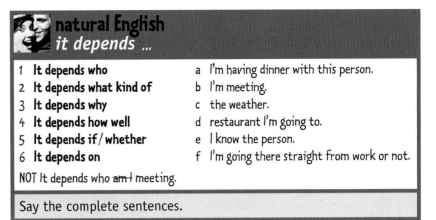

3 You're going to a wedding and you need to buy something to wear. With a partner, think of five sentences beginning *It depends …*

vocabulary clothes and dressing

1 Look at the pictures for 30 seconds, then shut your book. Tell your partner what everyone's wearing.

examples   There's a man wearing a suit.
There's a woman wearing jewellery.

suit /suːt/	tie /taɪ/	T-shirt	evening dress
tracksuit /ˈtræksuːt/	shorts	top	sandals
trainers /ˈtreɪnəz/	jewellery /ˈdʒuːəlri/		

2 Say who looks:

casually dressed	smartly dressed	scruffy ⓖ /ˈskrʌfi/
trendy	elegant	

3 With your partner, name ten items of clothing <u>not</u> in the pictures.

4 **Think!** Decide on your answers to these questions.

1 Which do you usually **put on** first – your shirt / top or your trousers / skirt?
2 What do you **take off** first when you go to bed?
3 How many times do you **get changed** during the day?
4 How often do you **get dressed up** and do you enjoy it?
5 Is it important what you **wear** to class? Why / why not?

5 Compare your answers in small groups, using the verbs in **bold**.

listen to this

tune in

1 You're going to hear Tom's true story about a party. Before you listen, use the phrases below to predict what the story is about.

neighbours /ˈneɪbəz/	Tom's father
Major /ˈmeɪdʒə/ and Mrs Wise	formal
a drinks party	fancy dress

2 (5.4) Listen to **part 1** of the story and check your ideas.

listen carefully

3 Read the summary, then listen to the whole story and fill the gaps.

At the party, the men were wearing _____ , and the women were wearing _____ . Major and Mrs Wise were dressed as _____ and _____ . Major Wise shouted, ' _____ !' After the party, Major and Mrs Wise never _____ .

> **listening booklet** *p.18 and p.19*

Major and Mrs Wise

listening challenge

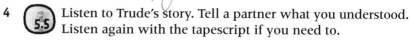

4 (5.5) Listen to Trude's story. Tell a partner what you understood. Listen again with the tapescript if you need to.

5 Have you ever worn the wrong clothes for an occasion? When? Why? What happened?

---

natural English
generalizations (1)

These phrases help to soften a statement or opinion.

Generally, I think most people wear scruffy clothes for that.
People **tend to** dress quite smartly for that.
It's not very common for people to wear very smart clothes.

Say the phrases.

---

6 Which sentences in the **natural English** box correspond to these situations?

1 going to a business meeting
2 going on a long train journey
3 painting a living room

it's your turn!

1 **Think!** Decide on your answers. Add one more situation yourself.

how do most people dress when they ...	
go for a job interview?	
meet their boyfriend / girlfriend's parents for the first time?	
come to their English class?	
travel to the beach?	
go to a concert or a play?	
your own situation	

2 Discuss all the situations in small groups.

🔊 **extended speaking**
Learn these phrases for later
It depends what kind of place it is.
People don't usually get dressed up.
People tend to go in groups.
It's not very common for people to ...

wordbooster

shopping

1 Fill the gaps with a form of the verbs from the box. Sometimes two verbs are possible.

pack	do	wait	order
attract	stand	push in	go
serve	put	get	

1 I get angry if shop assistants talk to each other while they're _____ customers.

2 When I _____ shopping for clothes, I always take a friend with me.

3 I don't always _____ the shopping; I take it in turns with the people I live with.

4 When people are queueing in a shop, it's not acceptable for others to _____ .

5 In some shops you can wait for ages trying to _____ someone's attention.

6 With some shops, you can _____ goods over the phone and they deliver them.

7 In supermarkets, shop assistants help you _____ your goods into carrier bags.

8 You have to _____ in a queue for about fifteen minutes in some shops.

2 In groups, make the sentences true for you in your country.

uses of *get*

A BUY / OBTAIN, E.G. YOU CAN GET A MEAL THERE

B RECEIVE, E.G. I GOT A LETTER TODAY

C ARRIVE / REACH, E.G. WE GOT TO THE AIRPORT AT 2.30

1 Match the sentences with one of the meanings of *get* above.

1 We can get something to eat here.
2 When you get the bill, you should pay it immediately.
3 Two beers, please. Oh, hi, Joe. Can I get you a drink?
4 You can get anything you want here.
5 We should get there by 10.00.
6 I never get phone calls after midnight.
7 When did they get home?
8 I couldn't get any crisps. They'd run out.

2 Complete the sentences in a suitable way.

1 If you're going to the chemist's, can you get _____ ?
2 What time did you get _____ ?
3 I'm always very happy when I get _____ .
4 Where did you get _____ ?
5 I checked my e-mails at lunchtime, and I got _____ .
6 I'm really hungry. I must get _____ .

how to... explain what to do

When you're giving instructions or explaining what to do, the modal verbs and phrases in this lesson are particularly common and useful.

vocabulary supermarkets

Match these words / phrases with items in the picture.

till	cashier /kæˈʃɪə/	shelves	checkout	goods
trolley	carrier bag /ˈkærɪə bæg/	basket	wheels /wiːlz/	

grammar obligation and permission

1 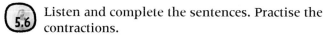 **5.6** Listen and complete the sentences. Practise the contractions.

1 You _____ your trolley over there.

2 You _____ the trolley home.

3 You _____ when people are queueing.

4 You _____ a shopping list.

5 You _____ your trolley in other people's way.

2 Match phrases 1 to 7 with definitions a to g.

1 you**'re allowed to / can** do it   a it's not necessary to do it

2 you **shouldn't** do it   b it's OK; you're permitted to do it

3 you **don't have to** do it   c it's necessary

4 you **mustn't** do it   d it's not permitted

5 you **should** do it   e it's not the right thing to do

6 you **have to** do it   f it's wrong, dangerous, or not permitted

7 you **aren't allowed to / can't do** it   g it's the correct / right thing to do

test your partner

– It's not necessary to do it.

– You mustn't do it.

– No, sorry, try again.

3 Think! What are the 'rules' of supermarket shopping in your country? Write T (true), F (false), or D (it depends) next to each sentence. If a sentence is false, change the verb in **bold** to make it true.

example

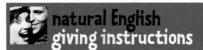

You can also pay by cheque or credit card.

SUPERMARKET SHOPPING DO'S AND DON'TS

xxxxxxxxxxxxxxxxxxxxxxxxxxxxxxxxx
24/01/02 12:11 2307 019 7427 4054
xxxxxxxxxxxxxxxxxxxxxxxxxxxxxxxxx

1 You're **allowed to** take dogs into a supermarket.

2 You **shouldn't** take things off the shelves yourself.

3 You **don't have to** pack the goods yourself.

4 You **should** buy a minimum of five things.

5 You **mustn't** eat the things in your basket before you get to the checkout.

6 You **aren't allowed to** smoke in the supermarket.

7 You **have to** pay by credit card.

8 You **mustn't** let children sit in your trolley.

9 You **have to** take a trolley.

10 You **don't have to** pay for carrier bags.

xxxxxxxxxxxxxxxxxxxxxxxxxxxxxxxxx
thank you - please call again
xxxxxxxxxxxxxxxxxxxxxxxxxxxxxxxxx

4 Compare your answers in small groups.

go to **language reference** *p.160*

look after a shop

1 Look at the photos. In your country, where can you buy these?

newspapers   cigarettes   soft drinks   sweets/chocolate   paper/pens

2 Imagine you're going to work in a local newsagent's. With a partner, think of three things you have to do/mustn't do.

3 (5.7) Listen. Which of your ideas did you hear? What other advice is given?

4 Listen again. Tick ✓ the phrases you hear in the **natural English** box.

natural English
giving instructions

The most important thing is to be polite.   **The first thing is to** switch it on.
Don't forget to shut the windows.   **Make sure** you lock the door.

Say the phrases.

listening booklet *p.18 and p.19 for tapescripts and exercises*

it's your turn!

In A/B pairs, A turn to *p.144* and B to *p.148*.

extended speaking
Learn these phrases for later
You don't have to ...   You aren't allowed to ...
You should always ...   You have to be 18 to ...

extended speaking

you're going to:

collect ideas
read about the way people behave in bars in Britain and California

focus on your country
decide how bars are similar / different in your own country

produce an information sheet
work in groups to write an information sheet about bars in your country

but first ...
Look back at the **extended speaking** boxes in this unit. You can use this language in the activity.

 collect ideas

1 In A / B pairs, A read 'pubs and bars in Britain' and B read 'bars in California'.

2 Shut your book, and tell your partner what you can remember.

3 Read your partner's information sheet to check the facts. Which facts do you find most interesting or strange?

EATING AND DRINKING

PUBS AND BARS IN BRITAIN

- You have to be 16 to go in a bar, but you're not allowed to drink alcohol until you're 18.

- Most traditional pubs have no waiters – you have to go to the bar to buy drinks.

- When you're in a group, you generally take it in turns to buy drinks for the whole group.

- You have to pay for each drink or **round of drinks** when they are served to you, and before you go and sit at a table. You can't usually pay for all your drinks together at the end of the evening.

- If you want to attract the attention of the bar staff, you shouldn't call out or **click your fingers**. The best thing is to hold some money up.

- Never offer the bar staff a **tip**, but you can buy them a drink if you like.

- You can get snacks such as crisps or peanuts, but they are not usually free. In some places you can also get a meal at lunchtime or in the evening.

- People tend to dress casually in bars; you don't have to dress up.

 glossary

round of drinks drinks you buy for everyone in your group

click your fingers make a sound with your fingers to get sb's attention

tip small amount of money you give for service

BARS IN CALIFORNIA

- You have to be 21 to enter or drink in a bar. If you look young, the **bartender** will ask to see your photo identity card.

- You can either sit at the bar or at a table, but you don't drink standing at the bar.

- If you sit at a table with waiter service, you don't have to pay each time you order; you can pay for all your drinks when you leave.

- Make sure you leave a **tip**: at least 15%.

- There are sometimes free nuts on the bar. If the bar doesn't serve food, you are allowed to bring your own snacks, or food can be delivered from a local restaurant.

- You aren't allowed to smoke in bars or any public places in California.

- You aren't allowed to drink alcohol in the street, so if you sit at an outside table, you can only drink coffee or soft drinks.

- Most bars have a TV showing sport, and traditional bars often have a pool table.

glossary

bartender (US) barman/barmaid (GB) man/woman who works in a bar

tip small amount of money you give for service

 ### focus on your country

4 Think! Look at both texts again and decide which points are true for your country. What other points could you add?

5 Work in small groups and compare your ideas.

 ### produce an information sheet

6 Read the checklist. In your group, write an information sheet for visitors to your country.

checklist
- Organize your ideas into a list of bullet points, as in the two texts.
- Include no more than ten bullet points.
- Before you start, look at the texts to find useful words and phrases you could use.

7 Find a partner from a different group. Tell them what information you've decided to include, and discuss any differences between your groups.

From this unit, write down:

1 three possible answers to *thanks / thank you*.

2 four things you can see in a supermarket, apart from the goods, e.g. *cashier*.

3 one verb to use in each phrase:
_____ *someone's attention*, _____ *in a queue*, _____ *the shopping*, _____ *shopping*.

Complete the sentences. The meaning must stay the same.

1 It's not necessary to do that.
You don't _____ .

2 Can you sit on the grass in this park?
Are you _____ ?

3 Don't forget to shut the windows.
Make _____ .

4 Are you a fast driver?
Do _____ ?

Correct the errors.

1 You haven't to do it now.

2 It depends how are you travelling.

3 Have you thought to give up smoking?

4 We all wear casually clothes here.

Look back at the unit contents on *p.57*. Tick ✓ the language you can use confidently.

a bad memory

how to ... react to a joke

That's quite funny.

I don't get it.

That's a good one.

That's an old joke.

That's terrible.

do you get it?

with a partner ...

Do you have a good memory? What do you find easy / difficult to remember? How do you remember things?

joke time

Look at the pictures. What's happening in each one? What's going to happen next?

6.1 Listen to the joke. Did you get it? Go to *p.20* of the listening booklet and listen again.

---

natural English
giving and responding to exciting news **6.2**

You'll never guess what's happened! I've won $1,000!	**What? You're joking!**
You won't believe who I've just met! Cameron Diaz!	**No, really?**

Listen and practise the dialogues. With a partner, invent and respond to news about your classmates:

_____ has won an Olympic medal.   _____ has just got married.

_____ has had a baby.   _____ is going to be on TV.

---

jobs in a company

Match the jobs to the definitions.

managing director	personnel /ˌpɜːsəˈnel/ manager
IT technician /tekˈnɪʃn/	factory supervisor /ˈfæktri ˈsuːpəvaɪzə/
financial controller	management consultant /kənˈsʌltənt/

1 a person who's in charge of the money in a company
2 a person who's in complete control of a company
3 a person who employs and trains people in a company
4 a person who looks after computers
5 a person who gives advice to companies
6 a person who checks people's work on the production line

test your partner

– A person who's in charge of the money in a company.

– Financial controller.

– That's right.

---

in unit six ...
tick ✓ when you know this

natural English

giving and responding to exciting news ☐
fortunately, hopefully, surprisingly ☐
I don't think (that) ... ☐
talking about advantages and disadvantages ☐
sort, kind, type ☐
ending a phone conversation ☐

grammar

sentences with *if, when,* and *unless* ☐
-ing form ☐

vocabulary

jobs in a company ☐
education ☐
agreeing and disagreeing ☐
course enquiries ☐

wordbooster

stages in a career ☐
learning phrases in sequences ☐

reading filling a gap

vocabulary education

1 Which noun in each row doesn't collocate with the verb in the first column? In one row, all three nouns are possible.

GO TO	school	~~language school~~	university
DO	a degree	a career	a course
TURN DOWN	an exam	an offer	a place at university
TAKE	a year off	research	an exam
LEAVE	school	home	university
GET	a grant	a qualification	a course

test your partner

– … a year off.

– That's right.

– Take a year off.

2 Think! Have you left school? If so, look at A below; if not, look at B.

A When you left school, did you study, get a job, or do something else? Why?

Which different options did you consider at the time?

Do you think it was the best thing to do?

B When you leave school, will you study, get a job, or do something else? Why?

Which different options are there for you?

3 Compare your answers in small groups.

grammar sentences with *if*, *when*, and *unless*

1 Read 'Hannah's choice', then answer these questions about sentences 1 to 4.

   a In sentence 1, what tenses are used? Is she sure that she'll get a job?

   b In sentence 2, what tenses are used? Is she sure she'll go to university?

   c In sentence 3, what tenses are used? Does *unless* mean *if* or *if + not*?

   d In sentence 4, there are two present simple verbs. Why?

   e In sentences 1 and 4, can you replace *if* with *when*, and keep the same meaning? Why / why not?

2 With a partner, practise your pronunciation. Read sentences 1 to 4 in 'Hannah's choice'.

3 Choose the correct form in these sentences.

   1 I'll decide what to do if / when I get my exam results.

   2 When / If I finish work on time tonight, I'll meet you for a drink.

   3 I'll lose my job if / unless the business starts to get better.

   4 I'll leave the company if / unless my boss gives me a pay rise.

   5 If / Unless I don't work late tonight, I might have to work on Saturday.

   6 If they offer / will offer me a good salary, I / I'll take the job.

   7 I / I'll leave at the end of the month if I don't / won't like this new job.

   8 If I don't / won't get the job, I don't / won't tell anybody.

4 With a partner, think of more consequences of Hannah's decision.

   examples
   If she gets a job near her home, …
   If she works abroad, …

5 Compare your ideas as a class.

go to **language reference** *p.162*

Hannah's choice

Hannah Lean is 17, and already has a place to study Psychology at university in October. However, she has a choice. She could:

- go to university this October.
- get a job near her home for a year, then go to university next October.
- work abroad for a year and then go to university next October.

At the moment, the second possibility sounds attractive. [1] If she gets a job and lives at home, she'll be able to save money. [2] That will help her when she goes to university. On the other hand, [3] she probably won't get another chance to live abroad unless she does it now. Hannah says, 'It's a difficult choice. [4] If I have to make big decisions, I always talk to mum and dad first. But in the end, I do what I want!'

read on

1 Read the beginning of the article. Find three things people in Britain do immediately after leaving school.

2 In A / B pairs, A read about Jim Edwards and B read about Ingrid Locke.

3 Tell each other what the person is going to do, and why. What do you think of their plans? Which would you do, and why?

>WHERE DO WE GO FROM HERE?

glossary
'A' level (Advanced level) public exams students usually take at 18 in Britain

MANY STUDENTS in Britain used to leave school at 18 and go straight to university to do their degrees without considering possible alternatives. Nowadays, things are different: 20% of students take a year off (the so-called 'gap year' between their **'A' level** exams and their university studies). Some stay in Britain and work during that year, but about half
05 want to go and work overseas. Other students choose a completely different route: they turn down university places in favour of finding permanent jobs. The advantage of this is that they can often study for professional qualifications in the company's time.

A >School-leaver JIM EDWARDS has decided to take a year off before going to university. He felt he wasn't
10 ready to **settle down** to university life immediately after finishing his 'A' levels. In a few weeks' time, he will be in Kenya, working on a marine wildlife project. 'It'll certainly be quite a culture shock at first, but I think I'll really enjoy working on the project and making new
15 friends,' says Jim. 'Fortunately, they speak English there, but I hope to learn the local language too.' He will earn very little money, but his food and accommodation will be free. **Eventually**, he is going to study Veterinary Medicine at Glasgow University.

B >INGRID LOCKE, 18, has now decided to start her career **instead of** going to university full time. She was offered a place at university to do a
25 degree in Hotel Management but, surprisingly perhaps, she turned it down. During the summer holidays, she worked
30 in a hotel which is part of a large group. The company were so impressed with her that they have offered her a permanent job, and the opportunity to
35 carry on studying one day a week to get qualifications in hotel management. 'They offered me the job the day before I finally had to decide
40 about university. Hopefully, I won't regret it,' says Ingrid.

glossary
settle down stay in one place, follow a conventional, routine life
eventually /ɪˈventʃuəli/ after a long time

glossary
instead of /ɪnˈsted əv/ in place of

4 Complete these sentences using the adverbs in the **natural English** box and your own ideas.

1 I'm going to spend six months in Germany; _____

2 I didn't have any money with me; _____

3 My uncle usually forgets my birthday; _____

4 It's a difficult situation, but _____

it's your turn!

1 **Think!** Imagine you're going to take a year off. What will you do? Read the possibilities and complete the table.

	yes/no/ not sure	reason
teach children in China to speak your language		
work as a waiter/ waitress on a cruise ship		
go to Australia and study English		
get business experience working for a bank		
organize sports activities for young people		
work for a company where you learn to design websites		
your own idea		

2 Compare your ideas in groups.

🔊 extended speaking
Learn these phrases for later
If that happens, they'll …
He won't be able to do that unless he …
Things will be very different when …
If he does a course, he might …

wordbooster

stages in a career

1 **Put the stages in A and B in a logical order. Compare with a partner.**

A ☐ you **give up your job**
☐ you **get a lot of experience** in the area
☐ you **set up** your own business
☐ you **borrow money** from the bank
☐ you **work for a company** for a few years
☐ you **apply for a job**
☐ you decide to **take a risk**
☐1 you **do a degree** in business studies

B ☐ you **look after** the baby
☐1 you **find a job** in the computer industry
☐ you **carry on working** for a few months
☐ you **settle down** and decide to **start a family**
☐ you **have a baby**
☐ you **go back to work**
☐ you **take six months off** work
☐ you **get married**

2 **You have two minutes. Learn one of the sequences in a logical order. Close your books and test each other.**

learning phrases in sequences

1 **Here is part of another common sequence. What important phrases can you add to the sequence? (If you don't know a phrase in English, write a translation.)**

you look at the adverts in a newspaper

_____

_____

_____

_____

you start your first job

2 **Compare your sequence with two other people. Add any new phrases and record them in your notebook.**

listening for and against

vocabulary agreeing and disagreeing

1 **Think!** Who of your friends and family do you usually agree / disagree with most?

2 Tell a partner.

3 Put the words in the speech bubbles in the correct order. Write contractions, e.g. *you're*.

4 Say the phrases.

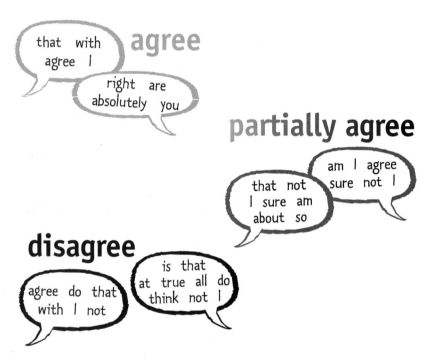

agree

> that with agree I

> right are absolutely you

partially agree

> that not I sure am about so

> am I agree sure not I

disagree

> agree do that with I not

> is that at true all do think not I

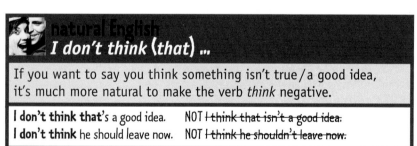

natural English
I don't think (that) ...

If you want to say you think something isn't true / a good idea, it's much more natural to make the verb *think* negative.

I don't think that's a good idea.	NOT ~~I think that isn't a good idea.~~
I don't think he should leave now.	NOT ~~I think he shouldn't leave now.~~

5 **Think!** Decide what you think about these statements.

a A career is the most important thing in life.

b I think studying is better than working.

c I don't think a boring job is better than no job.

d A good salary is necessary for job satisfaction.

6 Compare your ideas with a partner and agree / disagree.

listen to this

tune in

1 You're going to listen to Chris, who works in his father's company. Before you listen, look at a to g below. Decide which are advantages and which disadvantages of working in a family business.

a You work with people you know well.

b Bad business affects the whole family.

c Other employees may not trust you.

d There's less chance you'll lose your job.

e The company could be yours one day.

f Problems at work create family problems too.

g You may not feel fully independent.

2 (6.3) Listen to Chris. Which point does he make?

listen carefully

3 Listen to the whole conversation. Tick ✓ the other points Chris makes. In general, is he happy about his situation?

grammar -ing form

1 Circle the -ing forms in these sentences. What kind of word comes before -ing?

1 One advantage of speaking English is that it helps you get a job.

2 You should never give up your job before finding another one.

3 You should borrow money from friends or family instead of going to the bank.

4 You shouldn't set up a business without doing a management course first.

5 You should apply for jobs immediately after leaving school or university.

6 The disadvantage of working in only one company is that you don't get enough variety of experience.

go to **language reference** *p.163*

2 Mark a pause **‖** in the sentences and with a partner, read them aloud.

example
One advantage of speaking English **‖** is that it helps you get a job.

3 **Think!** Do you agree or disagree with the statements in **exercise 1**? What are your reasons?

4 Compare your ideas in small groups.

listening challenge

4 Catherine works freelance and does most of her work at home. Think about the advantages and disadvantages of her situation.

5 Listen and tell a partner what you understood. Listen again with the tapescript if you need to.

listening booklet *p.20 and p.21 for tapescripts and exercises*

natural English
talking about advantages and disadvantages

The main advantage of working in the family business is ...
Another advantage is ...
The disadvantage of my situation is ...

With a partner, use the phrases to talk about the advantages and disadvantages of working for a very big / very small company.

6 What's your opinion about working a) freelance b) in a family business? Do you or would you do it? Tell a partner.

extended speaking

Learn these phrases for later
You're absolutely right.
I'm not sure about that.
I don't agree with that at all.
The main advantage of doing that is ...

how to ... enquire about a course

If you're going to make enquiries, plan the questions in advance. This will help you to get the information you want, and give you time and confidence to focus on the answers you hear.

vocabulary course enquiries

1 Which words / phrases are connected with:

   a money?   b starting a course?   c the end of a course?

   enrol (v) /ɪnˈrəʊl/   pay a deposit   entry requirements (n)
   brochure (n) /ˈbrəʊʃə/   fees (n)   certificate (n) /səˈtɪfɪkət/
   application form (n)   qualification (n)

2 Underline the stressed syllables. Say the words / phrases.

3 **Think!** Read the questionnaire. What are <u>your</u> answers?

4 Compare your answers with a partner.

Your **English** course

1 Is your English course ☐ **full-time** or ☐ **part-time**?
   Do you prefer it like that? ☐ yes ☐ no

2 Is it ☐ a **one-month course**, ☐ a **nine-month course**,
   or something different?
   How long would you like it to be?

3 When did you **enrol on** the course?
   Are you enrolled on any other courses? ☐ yes ☐ no

4 Did you have to **pay fees** for this course? ☐ yes ☐ no
   If so, when?

5 Did you have to **pay a deposit**? ☐ yes ☐ no

6 Were there any **entry requirements** for the course? ☐ yes ☐ no
   For example, did you have to **take a test** before you started?
   If so, what did you think of it?

7 Does your school / college have a **brochure**? ☐ yes ☐ no
   If so, did you see it before you started the course?

8 Did you have to **fill in an application form** before you started?
   ☐ yes ☐ no
   If so, what information did you have to give?

9 What do you get at the end of your course:
   ☐ a **certificate**, ☐ a **qualification**, or ☐ nothing?

10 Would you like to **do** an exam **course** in English in the future?
   ☐ yes ☐ no
   If so, what?

phone for information

1 Matt has just left school. He saw this advertisement and wanted more information about computer courses.

City college

Courses commence:
July, September, January, & April

Accountancy
Business Studies
Computer Studies
Travel & Tourism
Hotel Management
Secretarial Studies

for further information

contact:

City college
24–28 Cornwell Rd
OXFORD OX2 8SL

01865 667724
info@citycoll.ac.uk
www.citycoll.ac.uk

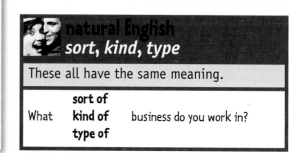

natural English
sort, kind, type

These all have the same meaning.

What	sort of kind of type of	business do you work in?

2 Complete the questions that Matt might ask the college receptionist. Add three more questions. Use the phrases in **bold** in the questionnaire on *p.76* to help you.

What kind of _____ ?

How long _____ ?

Do I have to _____ ?

3 Listen to the conversation. Does Matt ask the questions you wrote?

4 Listen again. Make notes in the table.

diplomas / qualifications?	yes
length of courses?	1 Sept to _____ 2 _____ to _____
starting date?	
hours per week?	
fees?	
deposit?	
class size?	
entry requirements?	school qualifications, basic computer skills
how to enrol?	

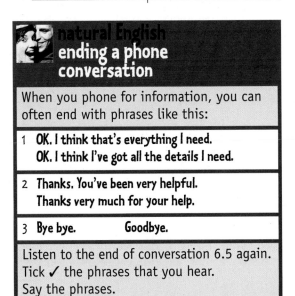

natural English
ending a phone conversation

When you phone for information, you can often end with phrases like this:

1 **OK. I think that's everything I need.**
  OK. I think I've got all the details I need.

2 **Thanks. You've been very helpful.**
  Thanks very much for your help.

3 **Bye bye.**   **Goodbye.**

Listen to the end of conversation 6.5 again. Tick ✓ the phrases that you hear. Say the phrases.

it's your turn!

1 In A / B pairs, A turn to *p.144* and B to *p.146.*

2 With your partner, ask and answer about your role play.

1 Did you have any problems asking questions?

2 Did you have any problems giving information?

3 Did you understand each other?

3 With the same partner, A turn to *p.149* and B to *p.150.*

complete an application form

1 Complete as much of this form as possible about a partner, without asking them.

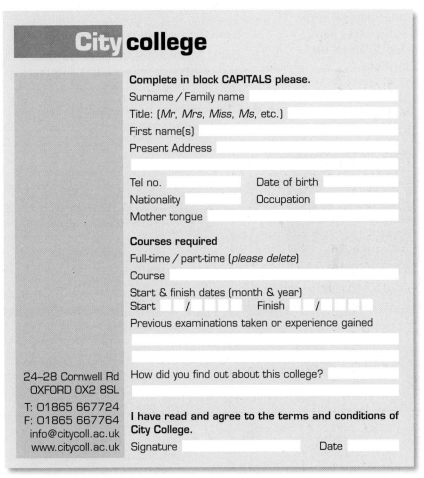

City college

Complete in block **CAPITALS** please.

Surname / Family name

Title: (*Mr, Mrs, Miss, Ms*, etc.)

First name(s)

Present Address

Tel no.   Date of birth

Nationality   Occupation

Mother tongue

Courses required

Full-time / part-time (*please delete*)

Course

Start & finish dates (month & year)
Start   /   Finish   /

Previous examinations taken or experience gained

How did you find out about this college?

I have read and agree to the terms and conditions of City College.

Signature   Date

24–28 Cornwell Rd
OXFORD OX2 8SL

T: 01865 667724
F: 01865 667764
info@citycoll.ac.uk
www.citycoll.ac.uk

2 Ask your partner questions to find out the information you couldn't complete and ask how to spell things.

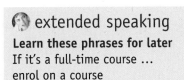

extended speaking

Learn these phrases for later
If it's a full-time course ...
enrol on a course

get a qualification in ...
What sort of ... is it?

extended speaking

you're going to:

collect ideas
read a true story about a couple who have to make an important decision

reach a decision
discuss the advantages and disadvantages of the options they have and decide on the best one

listen
find out what the couple's decision is

but first ...
Look back at the **extended speaking** boxes in this unit. You can use this language in the activity.

 ## collect ideas

1 **Think!** When you have to make an important decision (e.g. change jobs, end a relationship), do you:

  1 make the decision yourself or ask others for advice?

  2 think about it for a long time or make a quick decision based on your feelings?

2 Read the case study with the glossary.

3 **Think!** Make notes in the table on one or two advantages and disadvantages of each possible solution.

4 Compare ideas with a partner. Add any new ideas to your notes.

	advantages	disadvantages
1 photography business		
2 Rowena going back to work		
3 retraining in business		
4 moving to a different area		

CASE STUDY

Andrew and Rowena got married a year ago and are expecting a baby this year. Rowena has a well-paid job as an accountant, working in London (an hour away by train). Andrew has been working as an engineer in the **aviation industry** for ten years, but his company is closing down and there are no other similar jobs in the area. They'd like to stay in the same village, as the rest of Andrew's family are close by. They have to make a difficult decision. These are the ideas they have discussed so far:

1 Andrew enjoys photography very much, and has thought about starting a local photography business. There isn't much **competition** from other photographers nearby, but he will need to borrow money from the bank to start up the business.

2 Rowena could go back to work after the baby is born and be the main **breadwinner**. Andrew could stay at home and look after the baby.

3 Andrew could probably find a good job in the aviation industry, but they'll have to move to a different part of the country.

4 With his commercial experience, Andrew could retrain and go into business management: there's a one-year course at his local college. If he does that, he'll probably be on a low salary for a year or two after retraining.

glossary

aviation industry industry which makes aeroplanes

competition other people who want the same business as you and want to be more successful

breadwinner person who earns money to support the family

reach a decision

5 Work with another pair. Discuss the advantages and disadvantages of <u>each</u> solution. At the end, take a vote and decide on the best one.

6 Find a new partner. Say what your group decided, and why.

listen

7 Listen to Andrew. What have they decided to do?

8 Listen again. Are the disadvantages that Andrew and Rowena mention similar to your predictions in the table on *p.78*?

9 How many people in your group made the same final decision as Andrew and Rowena?

From this unit:

1 write the missing particle or preposition in these phrases: *look ___ a baby, give ___ a job, turn ___ an offer, carry ___ working, apply ___ a job, set ___ a business, the advantage ___ working, what sort ___ job?*

2 tell a partner this information about you: *your surname, nationality, date of birth, occupation, mother tongue.*

3 mark the stress on these words: *enrol, deposit, brochure, certificate, qualification.*

Complete the sentences. The meaning must stay the same.

1 We'll be late if we don't go now.
We'll be late unless _____ .

2 Thanks very much for your help.
Thanks. You _____ .

3 I think it's a bad idea.
I don't _____ .

4 I didn't go to work today.
I took _____ .

Correct the errors.

1 If they will move to another area, they will be unhappy.

2 I always feel better after go to the gym.

3 The main advantage to work there is the salary.

4 I'm not agree with you.

Look back at the unit contents on *p.69*. Tick ✓ the language you can use confidently.

love

life with Agrippine

with a partner ...

Describe your ideal boyfriend / girlfriend. Think about:

nationality	age	appearance	interests

cartoon time

Read the cartoon. What does Agrippine think of Trevor? What does her friend think of him?

 Listen and follow the cartoon. Then test your partner on the glossary words.

natural English
have a great / dreadful / good time

We **had a great time** at the beach. = We enjoyed ourselves very much.
I'm **having a dreadful time** at work.
Have a good time next week!

Say the sentences.
Did you have a good or bad time last week? Why? Tell a partner.

in unit seven ...
tick ✓ when you know this

natural English
have a great / dreadful / good time ☐
suggesting a change of topic ☐
do / did for emphasis ☐
anyway, so anyway ☐
time phrases in narrative ☐
commenting on a book or film ☐

grammar
verb patterns ☐
present tenses in narrative ☐

vocabulary
reporting verbs ☐
relationships ☐

wordbooster
people in your life ☐
phrases with *go* and *get* ☐

glossary

bum ⑥ /bʌm/ the part of the body you sit on

gorgeous ⑥ /ˈɡɔːdʒəs/ very attractive

dreadful /ˈdredfl/ very bad

fall in love with sb start to love sb

gossip (n) sb who enjoys talking about other people's private lives

tactless not diplomatic; saying things that upset people (opp **tactful**)

listening

handling relationships

vocabulary reporting verbs

1 Work with a partner. Decide what you would say in these situations.

example
Advise a friend to look for a new job.
'I think you should look for a new job.'

1 **Warn** a classmate not to go to the local nightclub.
2 **Persuade** a friend to go on holiday with you.
3 **Refuse** to help a stranger in the street to push his car.
4 **Offer** to help an elderly neighbour with her shopping.
5 **Suggest** that you and a friend go to the cinema tonight.

2 Work with a partner. Say the verbs.

> **advise** /əd'vaɪz/ say what you think is best
>
> **warn** /wɔːn/ point out a danger
>
> **persuade** /pə'sweɪd/ make sb do sth by giving reasons
>
> **refuse** /rɪ'fjuːz/ say 'no'
>
> **offer** /'ɒfə/ say you will do sth for sb
>
> **suggest** /sə'dʒest/ give sb an idea or plan

lead-in

1 Fill the gaps in the questionnaire with the verbs in red. Compare with a partner. Don't answer the questions yet.

2 **Think!** What would <u>you</u> do in each situation and why?

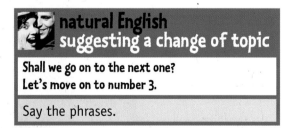

natural English
suggesting a change of topic

Shall we go on to the next one?
Let's move on to number 3.

Say the phrases.

3 Discuss your answers in groups. Use the phrases from the **natural English** box.

QUESTIONNAIRE

Should you be tactful or tell the truth?

1 You sent a present to your 14-year-old cousin, and she hasn't phoned or written to thank you. The next time you see her, two weeks later, she doesn't even mention the present.

Would you:

a [____] her you're upset?

b [____] to introduce the subject of the present into the conversation?

c [____] to say nothing?

d *your own idea*

| tell |
| decide | try |

2 Your 16-year-old brother tells you he's going to do a bungee-jump, without telling your parents.

Would you:

a [____] that it's dangerous?

b [____] him not to do it?

c [____] him that you'll tell your parents?

d *your own idea*

| advise |
| warn | explain |

3 Your best friend has to write a long essay on a subject she isn't very good at. She asks you to help her to write it.

Would you:

a [____] to help in the preparation, but not actually write it?

b [____] her to do it all herself?

c [____] to help?

d *your own idea* — persuade

| offer |
| refuse |

4 A classmate or colleague keeps interrupting when you're trying to work.

Would you:

a [____] him / her politely not to do it?

b [____] to him / her about it after class or work?

c [____] that he / she looks for a different desk?

d *your own idea*

| speak | tell | suggest |

5 You've decided you want to end your two-month relationship with your boyfriend / girlfriend.

Would you:

a [____] them face to face?

b [____] them and tell them it was over?

c [____] to them?

d *your own idea* — tell

| write | phone |

grammar verb patterns

1 Put the verbs in the correct part of the table.

explain	refuse	advise	tell	persuade	suggest
try	offer	realize	ask	warn	

verb + *that*
explain (He explained that he couldn't go.)

verb + *to do* sth
refuse (She refused to go.)

verb + sb *that*
warn (She warned me that he was angry.)

verb + sb + *(not) to do* sth
tell (Please tell Mark not to ring me.)

test your partner

– *Try …*

– *Try to do something.*

– *That's right.*

2 **Think!** Complete sentences 1 to 6.

1 ————————— me to go away.

2 ————————— to turn the radio down.

3 ————————— me that the bike wasn't safe.
4 I tried to persuade ————————— .
5 I advised ————————— .
6 My neighbour offered ————————— .

3 Compare your answers with a partner. How many of your sentences are the same?

go to **language reference** *p.163*

listen to this

tune in

1 🎧 **7.2** Look again at the questionnaire on *p.82*. You're going to hear extracts from two conversations. Listen and decide which situations in the questionnaire they relate to.

listen carefully

2 Listen to the whole of **conversation 2**. With a partner, answer the questions.

1 Why does the woman want to end the relationship?
2 Does the man sound angry?
3 What does he suggest?

3 **Think!** What's your opinion of the way the woman ended the relationship?

4 Compare your ideas with a partner.

listening challenge

5 🎧 **7.3** Listen to two women.

1 Which situation in the questionnaire on *p.82* does their conversation relate to?
2 How does the listener react?

If necessary, check your answers in the tapescript.

go to **listening booklet** *p.24 and p.25*

it's your turn!

1 Work with a partner. Choose one of the situations in the questionnaire.

1 Talk about the situation, and how each person could react.
2 Act out the conversation.

2 Act out your conversation for another pair. What do they think?

🔊 **extended speaking**

Learn these phrases for later
She realizes that they're …
He persuades her to …
He offers to …
She warns him not to …

wordbooster

people in your life

1 Match the words / phrases 1 to 8 with the definitions a to h.

1 relatives / relations
2 classmate
3 colleague /ˈkɒliːg/
4 neighbour
5 flatmate
6 ex-girlfriend / boyfriend
7 current /ˈkʌrənt/ boyfriend / girlfriend
8 best / closest friend

a sb you share a flat with
b e.g. cousins /ˈkʌznz/, uncles, nieces /ˈniːsɪz/
c sb you used to go out with
d sb who is in your class
e sb you know very well and like most of all
f sb you are going out with now
g sb who lives near you
h sb you work with

test your partner

– *Someone you used to go out with.*

– *That's right.*

– *Ex-boyfriend or ex-girlfriend.*

2 Write down the names of people in your life for five of the relationships in exercise 1.

3 With a partner, ask and answer about the names you wrote.

phrases with *go* and *get*

1 Match the words / phrases with the correct verb, *go* or *get*.

to know sb
on a date with sb
out for a drink / meal
on well / badly with sb
engaged / married / divorced
into trouble /ˈtrʌbl/
bankrupt /ˈbæŋkrʌpt/
wrong
out with sb
on holiday
angry / upset / excited / depressed
ready

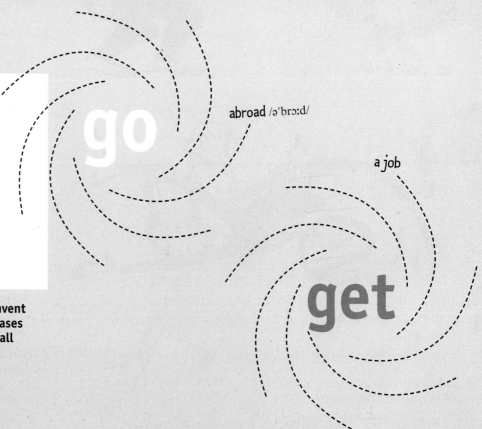

go

abroad /əˈbrɔːd/

a job

get

2 With a partner, take it in turns to invent sentences using two of the verb phrases in each. Continue until you've used all the phrases.

example
If I go abroad, I'll have to get a job.

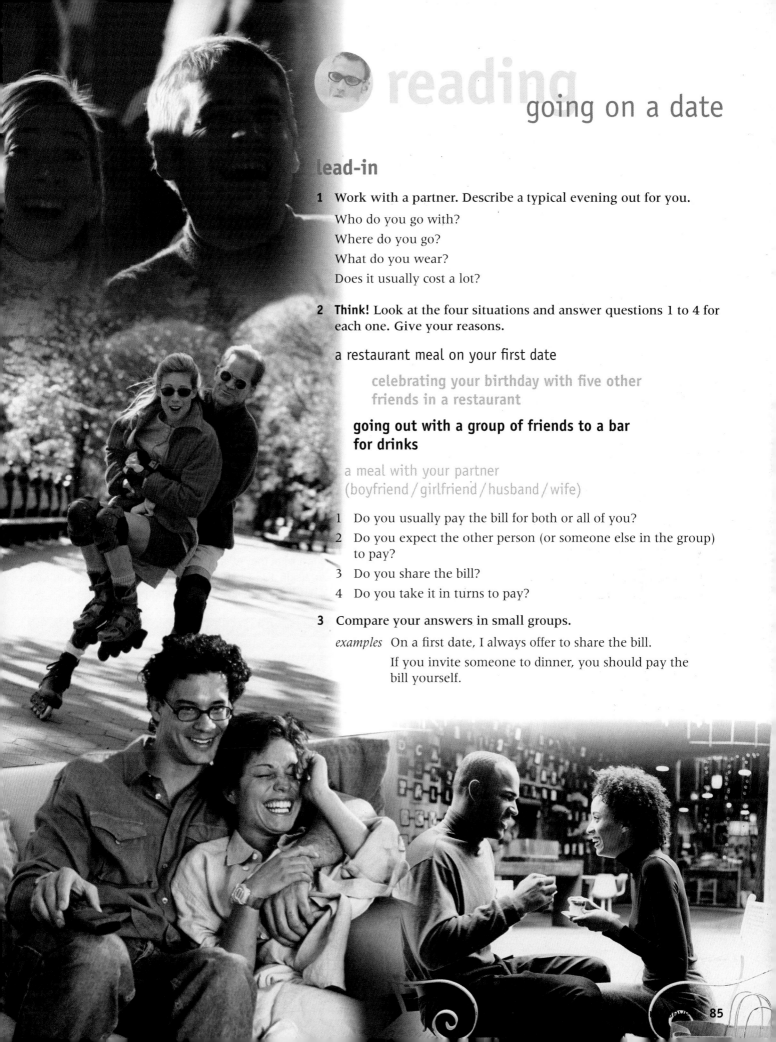

lead-in

1 Work with a partner. Describe a typical evening out for you.

Who do you go with?

Where do you go?

What do you wear?

Does it usually cost a lot?

2 **Think!** Look at the four situations and answer questions 1 to 4 for each one. Give your reasons.

a restaurant meal on your first date

celebrating your birthday with five other friends in a restaurant

going out with a group of friends to a bar for drinks

a meal with your partner (boyfriend / girlfriend / husband / wife)

1 Do you usually pay the bill for both or all of you?

2 Do you expect the other person (or someone else in the group) to pay?

3 Do you share the bill?

4 Do you take it in turns to pay?

3 Compare your answers in small groups.

examples On a first date, I always offer to share the bill.

If you invite someone to dinner, you should pay the bill yourself.

read on

1 Look at the photos with a partner. Decide what's happening.

example
A man's having a shave and he's …

language reminder
When describing what's happening in pictures, you usually use the present continuous.

2 Read the introduction to the story. Complete the title with *him* and *her*. Explain your reasons.

3 Which of these things do you think Sally and Joe did before or during the evening?

> made phone calls
> took a taxi to the wine bar
> put on make-up
> had a haircut
> bought drinks
> gave the waiter a tip
> bought clothes
> paid for dinner

4 Read the article with the glossary and check your ideas about Sally.

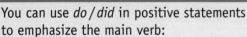

natural English
do / did for emphasis   (7.4)

You can use *do / did* in positive statements to emphasize the main verb:

I **do** feel sorry for that little child.
I like him and he really **does** work hard.
I **did** enjoy the film; it was brilliant!
I'm sure I **did** pay that bill.

Find examples in the text in paragraphs 2 and 4. Listen and say the examples. Stress *do / does / did*.

vowels a e i o u
consonants

We Went Halves

So why did it cost £103.64 for ☐ and £46.32 for ☐ ?

IT USED TO be customary on a date for a man to take the woman to the restaurant and take her home afterwards. And naturally, he paid the bill. But in our more egalitarian era, going on a date is much more complicated. Does the man offer to pay the bill or not? We asked a couple going on their
05 first date to note down what they each spent in preparation for the evening and on the evening itself. JOE CLARK is a 24-year-old architect who first met actress SALLY WHITE at a friend's party. Then he asked her out …

SALLY'S STORY

WHEN JOE invited me out to dinner, we agreed in advance to share the bill. My preparations do seem quite extensive, but the fact is, if you're a woman, they're pretty routine.
   … I looked through my wardrobe, phoned some of my friends to discuss what to wear and how to approach the evening. Eventually, I decided I'd need a new **outfit**, and I managed to find a black jacket that was quite cheap. Also, my hair was **a mess**, so I had to get it cut.
15 All of this took time and trouble, but I just wouldn't enjoy going out if I didn't feel confident about the way I looked. And of course, when I got ready, I put on make-up too.

glossary
go halves /hɑːvz/ share the cost of sth with sb
outfit (n) a complete set of clothes, e.g. top, trousers, and jacket
a mess ⓖ very untidy
set off start a journey
it turned out to be … I was a bit surprised to find it was …
it cost a fortune (figurative) it was very expensive

I was late **setting off**, and although I didn't have a lot of cash on me, I still took a taxi to the wine bar. **It turned out to be** miles from home so **it cost a fortune**! He was there waiting for me and we had a drink before the meal. Then we went to the restaurant and sat down. I noticed the food wasn't too expensive, which was reassuring.

Looking back, the meal was fine and we got on very well. At the end of it, Joe did offer to pay, in fact, but I refused. It's horrible when you're a woman and the man pays; it makes you feel less equal. However, Joe said he'd pay for the after-dinner liqueurs and he left a tip, which was fine by me.

Women know that in the end, these sorts of things always cost them more than men. It didn't surprise me in the least that, when we added it all up, I'd spent £103.64; more than twice as much as Joe. It isn't fair. But then, life isn't fair.

5 What do these phrases from the article refer to?

| her clothes? | her hair? | the meal? |

1 … we agreed in advance to share the bill …
2 … I looked through my wardrobe …
3 … I would need a new outfit …
4 … (it) looked a mess …
5 … I had to get it cut …
6 … he left a tip …

prepared
shared

6 What do you think of Sally's attitude to her evening out with Joe?

7 Listen to Joe's account of the evening. Are the statements true or false?

1 He chose a restaurant near his home.
2 He walked to the restaurant.
3 He had his hair cut.
4 He bought her a drink when she arrived.
5 His meal cost £35.
6 He really enjoyed the evening.

it's your turn!

1 **Think!** What's your opinion of the preparations Sally and Joe made? Would you do the same, or would you prepare differently? Make a list.

2 Compare your ideas with a partner of the same sex and, if possible, with someone of the opposite sex.

extended speaking
Learn these phrases for later
I think she's explaining something to him.
He's saying something about …
They're getting on very well.
… so anyway, when he …

how to ...
tell the story of a book or film

When you tell the story of a book or film in English, certain grammatical features and phrases are very common. You'll find these in this lesson.

vocabulary relationships

1 What was the last film you saw about a relationship? What was the relationship? What did you think of it? Tell a partner.

2 Match questions 1 to 5 with answers a to e. Say the phrases in **bold**.

1 Are they very involved with each other?
2 Is the relationship over?
3 Did they arrange to meet up?
4 Did they **have an argument**?
5 Do they **feel guilty**?

a No, they just **bumped into** each other at a party.
b Yes, they **had an awful row**.
c Yes, they've **split up**.
d Yes, they feel very bad about what they did.
e Oh, yes, it's **a serious relationship**.

test your partner
– Are they very involved with each other?
– Oh, yes, it's a serious relationship.

two film stories

1 You're going to listen to the beginning of the story of a film. Before you listen, decide how the sentences could end.

1 A man and a woman meet in a _____ .

2 They meet several _____ .

3 They eventually realize that they _____ .

4 The problem is that they are _____ .

2 Listen to the story and compare it with your sentences in **exercise 1**.

3 Listen to the whole of **story 1**. Complete the table.

the structure of the stories	They first meet in …	They realize that …	The problem is that …	The most important point is when …	At the end of the film …
story 1					
story 2					

4 Listen to **story 2**. Complete the table.

5 Do you recognize the two films? Have you seen them? If not, would you like to? Why / why not?

grammar present tenses in narrative

listening booklet *p.26 for the tapescript*

Look at the section of the tapescript in **bold** and answer these questions.

1 What tenses does Lynne use?
2 Do we always use these tenses when telling a story? Why is this kind of story different?
3 Change the verbs to the past. Which tense makes the story sound more immediate / exciting?
4 Does the same thing happen in your language?

go to **language reference** *p.164*

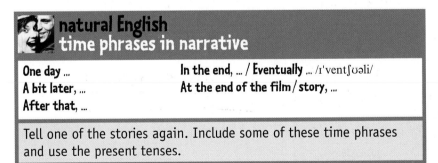

natural English
time phrases in narrative

One day …	In the end, … / Eventually … /ɪˈventʃʊəli/
A bit later, …	At the end of the film / story, …
After that, …	

Tell one of the stories again. Include some of these time phrases and use the present tenses.

it's your turn!

1 **Think!** Decide on a film, book, or TV drama you know which has an interesting relationship in it.

2 Make notes on the structure of your story and use the phrases from the **natural English** boxes.

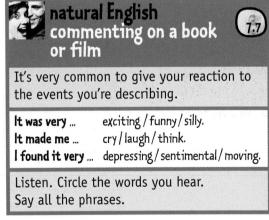

natural English
commenting on a book or film   7.7

It's very common to give your reaction to the events you're describing.

It was very …	exciting / funny / silly.
It made me …	cry / laugh / think.
I found it very …	depressing / sentimental / moving.

Listen. Circle the words you hear.
Say all the phrases.

3 Tell your stories in small groups.

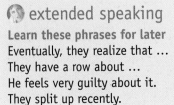

extended speaking
Learn these phrases for later
Eventually, they realize that …
They have a row about …
He feels very guilty about it.
They split up recently.

extended speaking

one couple's story

you're going to:

collect ideas
think about the characters of four people in a story

develop the story
decide on the story of how Sally and Joe's relationship develops

tell your story
tell your version of the story to another group

write the story
write your own version of the story

but first ...
Look back at the **extended speaking** boxes in this unit. You can use this language in the activity.

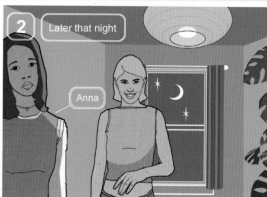

collect ideas

1 What can you remember about Sally and Joe from this unit? What are they like?

2 With a partner, look at pictures 1 to 8 and decide on your answers to the questions.

> **language reminder**
>
> When you talk about relationships, say 'Brian's mother', NOT 'the mother of Brian'.

> *go to* **language reference** *p.164*

  1 Who do you think Tom and Anna are?

  2 Look closely at the expressions on the faces of the four people. What do you think is happening in each picture?

  3 Will it work better as a dramatic, romantic, or funny story?

3 Compare your answers with another pair.

develop the story

4 Read this continuation of Joe and Sally's story. Which tense is used?

> Joe enjoys the evening at the restaurant with Sally, so he asks her out for another date. She agrees, and a few days later they meet at a club which she knows quite well. On this second date they get on really well, have a great time and end up dancing cheek to cheek. At the end of the evening Sally goes back to her flat and …

5 With a partner, develop the story. Make notes if you like, but don't write the story yet.

tell your story

6 Read the checklist, then practise telling the complete story with your partner.

checklist
- One of you should begin. Talk about two pictures, then the other can continue.
- Use the time expressions to help with the structure of the story.
- When you've finished, practise again to give you more confidence.
- Remember, you're going to tell someone else who doesn't know your story. Make sure the story is clear.

7 Work with a partner from a different group. Tell them your story and listen to theirs. Find two similarities and two differences. Ask if you don't understand anything.

write the story

8 With your original partner, start writing your version of the story. Finish it in your own time.

9 When you've finished, compare your versions.

eight

Bill Gates

glossary

client /ˈklaɪənt/ a business customer (the man in the green coat)

tap sb on the shoulder touch sb's shoulder to attract their attention (see the last picture)

how to ... react to a joke

- That's a good joke.
- That's very funny.
- I don't get it.
- I've heard it before.
- That's silly.

do you get it?

with a partner ...

What do you know about these people? What would you ask if you met one of them?

joke time

Look at the pictures. What's happening in each one? What's going to happen next?

8.1 Listen and react to the joke. Did you get it? Go to *p.28* of the listening booklet.

---

asking for help
8.2

Could you	do me a favour? /ˈfeɪvə/	Of course. What is it?
	give me a hand?	Sure.
	do something for me?	It depends what it is.

Listen and practise the dialogues.
Attract somebody's attention and ask them to do something for you.

---

getting people's attention

With a partner, do these actions.

example **A** Tap Mario on the shoulder.
B (do it)

| tap sb on the shoulder /ˈʃəʊldə/ | wave /weɪv/ at sb | catch sb's eye |
| call out sb's name | touch /tʌtʃ/ sb's arm | whistle /ˈwɪsl/ at sb |

in unit eight ...
tick ✓ when you know this

natural English
asking for help ☐
expressing difficulty ☐
prepositions at the end of *wh-* questions ☐
exclamations ☐
permission and requests ☐
introducing a question ☐

grammar
present continuous and *be going to* + verb ☐
talking about plans and arrangements ☐

vocabulary
getting people's attention ☐
everyday accidents ☐

wordbooster
everyday events in the home ☐
uncountable nouns ☐

93

 ## listening

adapting to a new lifestyle

lead-in

1 **Think!** Which of these would you find difficult to do? Why?
- drive on the left if you usually drive on the right
- work different hours from usual (e.g. at night, at the weekend)
- change to a completely different diet
- live in a country with a completely different climate
- live with people from a very different culture

 expressing difficulty

I'd **find it difficult / hard to** live in a very cold climate.
I **would have a problem** working different hours.
I **might have a problem** with that.

Say the phrases.

2 Compare your answers in small groups.

listen to this

tune in

1 (8.3) You're going to listen to Colin on the phone to a friend, Diana. Listen to the beginning of the conversation.

  1 Did Colin expect Diana to ring?   2 Does he sound pleased?

listen carefully

2 **Think!** Decide what kind of information could go in the gaps.

Colin works for ¹ _____ and they're sending him to Kazakhstan. He's leaving ² _____ , so when Diana invites him to dinner, he has to say no. On his first trip, he's going for ³ _____ , then after that, he'll spend one month at home and ⁴ _____ in Kazakhstan. To start with, he's staying in ⁵ _____ , but on later trips, he wants to ⁶ _____ . While he's there, he's hoping to ⁷ _____ .

3 Listen to the whole conversation. Complete the summary.

listening challenge

4 (8.4) Listen to the end of the conversation. What does Colin suggest? Tell a partner. Listen again if you need to.

listening booklet *p.28 and p.29 for tapescripts and exercises*

[map inset: RUSSIAN FEDERATION, MONGOLIA, KAZAKHSTAN, Almaty, CHINA, UZBEKISTAN]

grammar present continuous and *be going to* + verb

1 **Think!** Answer the questions.

   a <u>He's leaving</u> next Friday.

   b <u>He's staying</u> in a hotel to start with.

   c <u>He's going to look for</u> a flat when he's there.

   1 What tenses are the underlined phrases?

   2 How many of the plans are definite arrangements?

2 Compare your answers with a partner.

3 In which of these sentences could you also use the present continuous?

   1 My mother's going to arrive soon.

   2 They're going to rent a villa next summer.

   3 I'm going to find a hotel when I arrive.

   4 He's going to work hard tomorrow.

   5 I'm going to meet some friends for lunch.

go to **language reference** *p.165*

talking about plans and arrangements

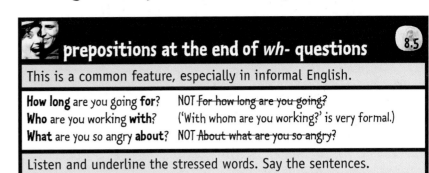

prepositions at the end of *wh-* questions   8.5

This is a common feature, especially in informal English.

How long are you going **for**?	NOT ~~For how long are you going?~~
Who are you working **with**?	('With whom are you working?' is very formal.)
What are you so angry **about**?	NOT ~~About what are you so angry?~~

Listen and underline the stressed words. Say the sentences.

1 Complete the sentences below with a suitable preposition.

   1 What are you going there _____ ?

   2 What kind of place are you staying _____ ?

   3 Which company are you going to work _____ ?

   4 Who else are you going _____ ?

   5 Is there anything you're worried _____ ?

2 **Think!** Choose a place you'd love to visit and imagine you're going to work there. Complete the table.

Your new life

questions	answers
Where? *Where are you going (to)?*	
When?	
How long?	
Why?	
Where staying?	
Free time?	
Worries?	

3 Find a partner. Ask them about their plans and arrangements.

giving advice

1 Read what Colin wrote to a friend. What are his main worries? Shut your book and tell a partner.

> ... THE MAIN THING I'M WORRIED ABOUT IS THAT I KNOW SO LITTLE ABOUT THE COUNTRY; I DON'T EVEN KNOW MUCH ABOUT THE CITY I'M GOING TO, OR THE LOCAL CUSTOMS. THERE'S ALSO THE PROBLEM OF LANGUAGE (WHICH OF COURSE I DON'T SPEAK). I SUPPOSE I MIGHT FEEL A BIT LONELY AND ISOLATED, AND I DON'T KNOW WHAT TO DO ABOUT THAT. I DON'T WANT TO JUST SPEND ALL MY TIME WORKING, BUT ...

2 What can Colin do before he goes, or when he gets there? Complete the sentences.

1 The best thing is for him to _____
_____ .

2 I'd advise him to _____
_____ .

3 I think he should _____
_____ .

4 I'd recommend _____ (-ing)
_____ .

3 Work in small groups. Listen and respond to other people's ideas.

🎧 extended speaking

Learn these phrases for later
They'd find it hard to ...
How long are they going for?
I think she should ...
I'd recommend going to ...

reading
living in the dark

vocabulary everyday accidents

1 Match the verbs and pictures. Are the verbs regular or irregular?

a trip over sth   d crash into sth   g drop sth
b spill sth   e bump into sth / sb   h knock sth over
c fall off sth   f step on sth / sb's foot

2 For picture 1, you'd say 'the woman has spilt her coffee on the table'. Why do you use the present perfect here and not the past simple?

3 With a partner, describe what has happened in the other pictures. Have any of these things happened to you recently?

go to **language reference** *p.166*

read on

language reminder

When you're making general predictions about the future, you can often use both *will* and *be going to* in English without any difference in meaning.
Who do you think will win the match?
Who do you think is going to win the match?

1 You're going to read an article about a restaurant where people have to eat their meal in total darkness. Make predictions using the sentence beginnings.

1 The customers will probably find it difficult to ...
2 They're going to have a problem ...
3 They won't be able to ...

go to **language reference** *p.165*

2 Read the article. Underline five problems the customers had.

3 Read the article again.

    1 Why is the restaurant so popular?

    2 Why did the owner want to open it?

    3 What are the 'rules' of the restaurant?

    4 How do the customers feel before and after the meal?

    5 Which of your predictions in **exercise 1** are mentioned?

4 Would you like to go to this restaurant? Why / why not?

expressing your feelings

1 Look at paragraphs 3 and 6. Underline any exclamations.

example (para 3)
<u>Oh, no</u>, I've spilt raspberry juice on my shirt!

---

exclamations   8.6

to express pleasure	Ah! Great! Ooh! _____!
to express surprise	What? _____!
to express pain	Ow! _____!
to express anger	Oh no!
when something bad has happened	Oh no! _____!

Listen and write these examples in the gaps above. Say the exclamations. How do you say them in your language?

Ouch!   Oh!   Oh dear!   Wow!

🔊 extended speaking

Learn these phrases for later
They'll probably find it difficult to ...
They won't be able to ...
They're going to have a problem ...

EAT IN THE
darkest
RESTAURANT IN PARIS

In Paris there's a new place to eat, and it's full every night. The chairs are plastic and the tablecloths aren't very clean, but
05 Parisians queue up to go there because it's a unique dining experience; it shows customers what it's like to be **blind**.

The restaurant is in total darkness, and dinner is served by blind waiters.
10 The customers aren't told what they're going to eat. They have to feel for their **cutlery** and glass on the table, and eventually they have to get up and serve themselves for the dessert course.

15 'Oh no, I've spilt raspberry juice on my shirt! Or is it chocolate sauce?' said one customer last week. 'Ow, you've just stepped on my foot!' said another.

The original idea was to help people
20 understand what it's like to be blind. However, the owner is delighted that the 'Goût du Noir', has been so successful. It's also shown that strangers become less reserved and
25 more open with each other when they get together in the dark. The customers who arrived on Friday night, for example, looked shy and nervous at first, but by the time they

30 left 90 minutes later, many were laughing and **hugging** new-found friends. 'Oh, that was exciting!' said one man. 'Wait,' said his wife, 'I've got to find Stéphane. I was sitting next to
35 him and I just have to know what he looks like.' Stéphane came out of the dark and the strangers fell into each other's arms.

Before each dinner begins, the owner
40 explains the rules. 'Please don't light a match or use your cigarette lighters. If you have any problems with the darkness, ask one of the waiters for help.' The first table of guests then
45 hold hands and are shown to their table.

'I can't see anything,' said a voice. 'Oh no, I've dropped my fork!' said another. 'Ouch! I've kicked a chair.' By the time
50 the third table was seated there was a lot of nervous laughter. 'Where's the wine?' asked someone. 'Oh, no, I've knocked it over!' came the reply. 'Oh dear, and I've just put my fingers in
55 someone's glass!' said another.

'For once,' said the owner, 'it's the blind who are showing the rest of us the way. The roles have been reversed.'

glossary

blind /blaɪnd/ unable to see

cutlery /ˈkʌtləri/ general word for knives, forks and spoons

hug /hʌg/ put your arms round sb

wordbooster

everyday events in the home

1 Match verbs and nouns/phrases to form common combinations.

make	the iron
invite	a meal for yourself
pay	a programme
borrow	the furniture around
hang	a friend over
send/receive	overseas phone calls
video	a picture on the wall
use	e-mail messages
move	the washing machine
cook	the rent late

test your partner

– Make ...

– overseas phone calls.

– That's right.

2 Would you let a guest staying in your house do the things above?

example

A Would you let them make overseas phone calls?

B Yes, I would. How about you?

uncountable nouns

1 Correct the mistakes.

1 We had a good weather on our holidays.
2 They gave us some good advices.
3 Our accommodation were horrible.
4 The informations we got didn't help.
5 I couldn't do the homeworks last night.
6 We left our luggages in reception.
7 The traffic were very bad this morning.
8 There's a news of a bank robbery in Paris.

2 List the nouns in exercise 1 which are uncountable in English and countable in your language.

go to **language reference** *p.166*

how to ... be a good guest!

When you're making requests in English, longer questions can often sound more polite, and intonation is important too. Asking the right question can help.

ask for and give permission

1 Think! Decide on your answers to the questions.

1 When did you last stay in someone else's home?
2 Whose home was it, and why were you there?
3 Do you feel relaxed staying in other people's homes?
4 If you're staying with someone, what kind of things do you usually have to ask permission for? (e.g. use the phone)

2 Compare your answers with a partner.

---

permission and requests

Could I use your pen?
Do you mind if I borrow your dictionary?
Do you think I could leave early today?
Would you mind if I opened the window?
('Do you mind if I ... ?' means 'Is it a problem for you if I ... ?')

Say the phrases. Ask permission to do two more things.

---

3 (8.7) Listen and complete the dialogues.

1 **A** Could I borrow the iron, please?
  B _____ .
2 **A** Do you mind if I use the washing machine?
  B _____ .
3 **A** Do you think I could make a phone call?
  B _____ , as long as it's quick. I'm expecting a call.
4 **A** Would you mind if I cooked something for myself?
  B _____ , go ahead.

go to **listening booklet** *p.30 and p.31*

4 Why do we answer 'yes' in some questions, and 'no' in others? Practise the dialogues with a partner.

5 You're staying at a friend's house. Look at the photos opposite. Act out short dialogues with a partner for each one.

A ask for permission to use/do something

B give permission, or say 'I'm sorry', and then give a reason

house rules

1 (8.8) You're going to listen to Trude, a German student who has just arrived to stay with her American landlady, Mrs Clark. Tune in to the beginning of the conversation.

1 Trude has done something. What is it?
2 Is Mrs Clark angry?

2 Listen to the whole conversation. Circle the correct answer.

1 Trude wants to check her e-mails / surf the Internet.
2 Mrs Clark / Mrs Clark's husband uses the computer.
3 Mrs Clark gives her permission / doesn't give her permission.
4 Trude usually has coffee and bread / fruit juice and cereal for breakfast.
5 Trude seems happy / unhappy with the arrangements.

---

natural English

introducing a question

Use these phrases to introduce a question that's important to you, or you've been planning to ask. The past simple / *was going to* sound a little more polite here.

I was going to ask you ... do you have a car?
I wanted to ask you ... can I use your hairdryer?
There's something I want to ask you ... is there a bus from here into town?

Say the sentences.

---

go to **listening booklet** *p.30 and p.31*

3 Which phrase in the **natural English** box do they use?

4 With a partner, practise the section of the tapescript in **bold** until you can say it fluently.

it's your turn!

1 In A/B pairs, A turn to *p.145* and B to *p.147*.

2 With the same partner, swap roles. A turn to *p.149* and B to *p.150*.

write a message home

Imagine you're studying in London. Write an e-mail to your English teacher back home. Say what your landlord / landlady is like and describe the accommodation.

To ...	
Subject:	

Hello _____
Well, I've arrived safely and I'm now at my landlady's place. The journey was fine and ...

visitors to your country

you're going to:

collect ideas
look at the profiles of some different kinds of language learners

discuss in more detail
talk about the problems they might have learning your language

plan an information sheet
think of practical advice for foreign visitors to your country

write an information sheet
write an advice and information sheet to help them

but first ...
Look back at the **extended speaking** boxes in this unit. You can use this language in the activity.

collect ideas

1   Ask and answer these questions with a partner.

1   Do foreign visitors come to your town / area? If so, which nationalities?

2   What do they come for?

3   Do you ever meet them? If so, how and where?

2   In A / B pairs, A read about David, Mike, and Alex and B read about Rebecca.

3   Tell your partner what you read.

4   Read the other text. Did your partner tell you everything?

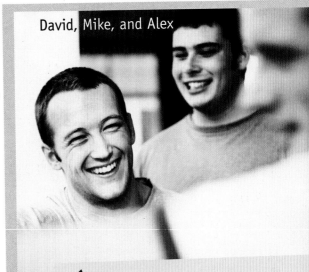

David, Mike, and Alex

↑ *These university students, David, Mike, and Alex, are studying Economics in Canada, and have got a grant to study your language in your town / city for six months. They'll be at language school or college every morning, and their level at the moment is elementary (lower than your level of English). They're all going to live with local families and it is the first time they've been to your country.*

Rebecca

↖ *This is Rebecca, who is a British business woman in her mid-forties. She's going to stay in a hotel in your town / city for three months and study your language at a language school or college, but she's paying for herself. She'll also spend some of the day working part-time in a company. Her level in your language is intermediate (about your level in English). In the future she hopes to do a lot of business with companies in your country. She hasn't been to your town / city before, but has been to your country on short business trips.*

discuss in more detail

5 Think! Decide on your answers to these questions.

1 What are the most important differences between Rebecca's situation and the three students' situation?

2 What specific problems with your language and customs might Rebecca and the students have?

3 Who do you think has the best chance of making progress in your language? Why?

4 What advice would you give someone coming to study in your country, to help them make the most progress?

6 Compare your answers in small groups. Then tell the class who you think will learn the most, and why.

 plan an information sheet

7 Think! Read the checklist.

– Imagine what it's like for someone who doesn't know your town or country. Think about:

public transport	eating out	entertainment
sightseeing	festivals	appropriate behaviour
changing money	opening / closing times	

– Decide if there are any other important things a foreigner needs to know.
– Think about foreigners you know or have heard about who have had problems.

8 Compare your ideas and make notes in small groups.

 write an information sheet

9 Work with a partner.

1 Choose two or three of your pieces of general advice.

2 Choose one piece of advice about learning the language.

3 Write them out as an information sheet.
   example

INFORMATION ABOUT BOLOGNA

1 If you're going to travel round town a lot, the first thing you'll need is a bus ticket. You can buy a citypass valid for ten journeys at any tobacconist's. You can use them on any bus in the city.

2 If you want to eat out, there are lots of excellent pizzerias and restaurants. We would particularly recommend a pizzeria called 'La Mela' near the main square. There are a lot of cheap places to eat in the university area too.

3 ...

10 Show your information sheet to another pair. What did they find most useful? Why?

From this unit, write down:

1 four ways of getting somebody's attention, e.g. *wave at* sb.

2 the complete phrasal verbs: *trip* _____ sth, *bump* _____ sth / sb, *fall* _____ sth, *crash* _____ sth, *knock* sth _____ .

3 three ways of asking for permission, e.g. *Could I open the window?*

Complete the sentences. The meaning must stay the same.

1 I'd find it difficult to do that.
   I'd have a problem _____ .

2 Could you help me?
   Could you do _____ ?

3 I think he should stay.
   I'd advise _____ .

4 Who do you think will win the game?
   Who do you think is _____ ?

Correct the errors.

1 Thank you for the very useful informations.

2 For how long are you going?

3 I go to the cinema tonight with my sister.

4 Oh no! I lost my wallet!

Look back at the unit contents on *p.93*. Tick ✓ the language you can use confidently.

transport

life with Agrippine

in groups ...

When did you last stay out late? Where did you go, who with, and how did you get home? What's public transport like late at night where you live?

cartoon time

Read the cartoon. Why does Agrippine tell her mother about the transport problems in such detail?

Why does her mother agree to drive her?

9.1 Listen and follow the cartoon. Then test your partner on the glossary words / phrases.

natural English
vague and exact time

Have you got the time?	What time do you make it?
It's **getting on for** seven. = nearly seven o'clock	Seven o'clock **exactly**.
Seven**ish** / eight**ish**, etc. = about 7.00 / 8.00	When shall we meet?
It's **around / about** six.	Six **on the dot**.

Say the phrases. What's the time now?

When do you do these things during the week / at weekends?

get up	have lunch	start work / college	have dinner	go to bed

glossary

hitch / hitchhike (v) /ˈhɪtʃhaɪk/ stand by the road and try to get cars to stop and take you somewhere

on the dot ⑤ exactly

drop sb take sb to a place you are driving past

pick sb up collect sb in your car

tractor /ˈtræktə/ transport used on farms

give sb a lift take sb somewhere in your car

reading

getting nowhere fast

lead-in

1 Work with a partner. Look at the headline and the photo.

  1 Explain what *rush hour, jam,* and *stuck* mean. Say the words.

  2 What do <u>you</u> do when you're stuck in a rush hour jam?

2 **Think!** Answer the questions to prepare your story.

  1 When was the last time you were stuck in a bad traffic jam?

  2 Who were you with and where were you going?

  3 How long did the journey take?

  4 How did you feel? Did it create any serious problems for you?

3 Tell your stories in small groups. Who had the worst experience?

vocabulary collocation

1 Make a list of things people do when they're stuck in a jam, using the verbs below.

example use your mobile phone

use	comb /kəʊm/	have	put on
do	scratch	sing	get
chat	stare /steə/		*your own ideas*

2 Compare with a partner.

read on

1 Read the article with the glossary. Match the people in the text with these personality types.

~~The Philosopher~~	Mr Take It Easy
The **Workaholic**	Mr Stressed
The Escapist	Miss Busy

2 Compare your list in **vocabulary exercise 1** with the phrases in the article.

3 Which person are you most similar to in the text? Which of the things do you do? Tell a partner.

What do <u>you</u> do when you're stuck in a rush hour jam?

Morning rush hour. In ten minutes you've moved just 100 metres. Yes, you're in a traffic jam. **AGAIN.**

05 Incredibly, one in five motorists spends five hours a week (that's 11 days a year) **crawling** along in a traffic jam. That's an awful lot of 10 spare time, so what do people do? From a survey of motorists, here are a few answers.

1

'I listen to the radio, but if I had a Rubik's cube, I'd play 15 with that,' said 27-year-old **Jeremy Kain**. 'I often get really angry because I'm a very punctual person, and I can't stand being late. I smoke 20 nothing the rest of the time, but twenty a day when I'm driving. I can't do anything constructive because I'm in such a bad mood.'

---

glossary

Complete with words from the article.

workaholic /wɜːkəˈhɒlɪk/ sb who can't stop working

crawl /krɔːl/ move very slowly

a _____ (adj) (part 1) arriving at the exact time you arranged

b _____ (part 1) feel angry/unhappy for a period of time

c _____ (part 3) have an informal conversation

d _____ (part 5) think about nice things to forget about real life

test your partner

– *Someone who can't stop working.*

– *A workaholic.*

– *That's right.*

2

25 **Sam Kumar**, 29, said: 'I think about work occasionally, but most of the time, I pretend I'm somewhere else – 30 somewhere miles away. I also comb my hair in the mirror, and I like to have a quick look at the paper.'

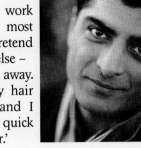

3

35 **Louise Foster**, 31, admitted to all sorts of things: 'I put on make-up in the mirror, I use my mobile phone all the time to chat to friends, I sing to myself, I listen to music,' she said. 'Just the other day I saw a 40 man having a shave.' She also agreed that the traffic drives her mad.

4 The Philosopher

Some people are more fatalistic. 'As a bus driver you have to be 45 tolerant,' said **Martin Thorburn**. 'I do get annoyed but there isn't much I can do about it. Some of the 50 time I just listen to the radio. We all scratch our heads and stare at ourselves in the mirror, don't we?'

5

Diane Gibbs drives a lot, and when she's 55 stuck in traffic she finds it difficult to relax. 'I'd like to daydream but I almost always think about work,' said Diane. 60 'I work on the phone a lot of the time and occasionally I do a crossword if I'm stationary.'

6

Steve Scott, a van driver, said: 'The traffic 65 doesn't bother me. I just listen to the radio and watch people walk by.' But then he added: 'I seem to spend my whole life in traffic jams.'

---

1 Match 1 to 3 with a to c in the **natural English** box. Where does each pair of phrases go on the line?

2 Complete the sentence using one of the phrases in the **natural English** box to make it true for you.

_____ if people park on the pavement.

1 Why should you use the present simple in both parts of the sentence here?

2 Which word could you use in place of *if*?

3 Tell a partner how <u>you</u> feel about the people's behaviour in the picture, using the **natural English** phrases.

example
A I can't stand it if people park on the pavement. I really hate it!
B Do you? It doesn't bother me.

4 Think of something you can't stand in any situation. Tell others in the class and see what they think.

extended speaking
Learn these phrases for later
It annoys me if people …
It doesn't bother me if …

I find it slightly irritating.
I'm always very punctual.

listening
how quickly do you do it?

lead-in

1 Do you like to be busy all the time, or do you take life at a relaxed pace? Which character in the picture is most like you?

2 Choose five topics. Compare with a partner how quickly or slowly you do them.

buy new clothes

choose what to wear in the morning

have lunch

have a shower or bath

tidy up your room / home

clean your teeth

do homework

buy a present for someone

have breakfast

get ready for bed

natural English
saying how quickly you do things

	quickly	slowly	
(I do it)	as quickly as possible	I spend a lot of time	
	in a rush /rʌʃ/	I spend ages	(doing it)
	in a hurry /'hʌri/	I like to take my time	

Say the phrases.

listen to this

	1 DeNica	2 Tyler	3 Julia	4 Patience	5 Jeff	6 Ralph
topic?						
how quickly / slowly?						

tune in

1 *(9.2)* You're going to listen to four people talking about how quickly they do some of the things in **lead-in exercise 2**. Listen to DeNica and complete the table.

listen carefully

2 Listen to Tyler, Julia, and Patience and complete the table.

listening challenge

3 *(9.3)* Listen to two more people, Jeff and Ralph, and complete the table. Listen again with the tapescript if you need to.

listening booklet *p.32 and p.33 for tapescripts and exercises*

grammar first and second conditional

1 Look at the examples. Answer the questions.

If I <u>had</u> more time,	I <u>could have</u> a nice, long lunch. I'<u>d go</u> out for lunch.
If I <u>earned</u> lots of money,	I'<u>d be able to</u> pay a cleaner. I <u>might pay</u> someone to tidy up.

1 What tense is used in the 'if' clause?
2 What verb forms are used in the second clause?
3 Are they talking about the past, or the present and future?
4 Is it possible at the moment for them to have more time or money?
5 Are they describing something real or imaginary?

2 Practise saying the sentences. Make up your own sentences beginning, 'If I had more time …' / 'If I earned lots of money …'.

3 Compare these sentences. Which 'if' clause will possibly happen, and which almost certainly won't? What tenses are used in these examples?

a If I had more time, I could have a nice, long lunch. ('second' conditional)

b If I have some free time this weekend, I'll give you a ring. ('first' conditional)

c If I earned lots of money, I might pay someone to tidy up.

d If I earn enough money next year, I'll probably get a new car.

4 Decide whether the 'if' clauses are possible or improbable. Fill the gaps.

1 It might be nice tomorrow. If it _____ (be) sunny, we _____ (go) to the seaside.

2 My father is in Iceland at the moment. If he _____ (be) here, I _____ (tell) him what has happened.

3 The flights are quite reliable. If we _____ (arrive) on time, we _____ (get) to your house by seven.

4 I'm incredibly busy. If I _____ (have) time, I _____ (help) you, but I'm afraid I can't.

5 The station is only a few minutes' walk. Come on, if we _____ (run), we _____ (catch) the train.

6 If I _____ (speak) Italian well, I _____ (apply) for that job in Rome, but I've only had a few lessons.

go to **language reference** *p.167*

talk about your daydreams

1 Look at the table. Add your own ideas. Tick ✓ your top five.

I'd like to have ...

- ☐ more free time
- ☐ more money
- ☐ less homework
- ☐ more English-speaking friends
- ☐ less responsibility
- ☐ more opportunity to travel
- ☐ *your own idea* _____

I'd like to be ...

- ☐ taller
- ☐ older / younger
- ☐ the opposite sex
- ☐ in a rock group
- ☐ famous
- ☐ the president / leader of my country
- ☐ *your own idea* _____

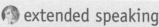 **natural English**
if I was / were ...

In *if* clauses in spoken English, you can say *was* or *were* with *I*, *he*, and *she*.

If I	**was** /wəz/	younger, the job would be easier.
	were /wə/	

Was is more informal; *were* is more formal.

2 Write sentences about the things you ticked in **exercise 1**.

examples
If I had more time, I'd / I wouldn't ...
If I was / were taller, I could ... / I might ...

3 Ask others what they wrote and why.

it's your turn!

1 **Think!** Look at imaginary situations 1 to 4. Complete the first one, then think of a positive and negative consequence for each situation.

What would happen if ...

1 public transport ran 24 hours a day?

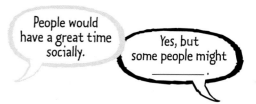
People would have a great time socially.

Yes, but some people might _____.

2 everyone lived to be exactly 100?

3 you had to work for three years before going to university?

4 everyone could only work part-time?

2 Compare your ideas in small groups. Choose the best idea.

🔊 **extended speaking**

Learn these phrases for later
I do it in a hurry.
I spend ages doing it.

If you arrived late, would you ...?
What would you do if ...?

wordbooster

words often confused

1 Choose the best ending (c or d) for the sentence beginnings (a and b).

1 a They **cancelled** the party   c until the following week.
    b They **postponed** the party   d and went out instead.

2 a She didn't arrive **in time**   c so her interview started late.
    b She didn't arrive **on time**   d so she caught the next train.

3 a He was late for the **meeting**   c with his colleagues.
    b He was late for the **date**   d with his new girlfriend.

4 a The letter wasn't **urgent**   c so she threw it in the bin.
    b The letter wasn't **important** d so she didn't reply immediately.

5 a She's always very **punctual**; c she'll be here by 3.00.
    b She's always very **reliable**;   d she'll do a good job.

test your partner

– *He was late for the meeting …*

– *… with his colleagues.*

– *That's right.*

2 Think! Complete the sentences with your own ideas.

1 I always _____ on time.

2 _____ is very punctual.

3 _____ isn't very reliable.

4 I'd like a date _____ .

5 I'd be unhappy if they cancelled _____ .

6 The last meeting I went to _____ .

Compare with a partner.

prefixes

1 Use a prefix to make these adjectives negative. Say the adjectives.

1 [ ] ····· logical

2 [ ] ····· efficient

3 [ ] ····· practical

4 [ ] ····· honest

5 [ ] ····· fair

6 [ ] ····· responsible

7 [ ] ····· pleasant

8 [ ] ····· organized

9 [ ] ····· convenient

10 [ ] ····· patient

2 Do you have prefixes in your language? If so, which are the same, and which are different?

3 Complete the sentences with a suitable word from exercise 1.

1 Mike and I do the same job, but he earns more. It's very _____ !

2 The bathroom is very _____ because it's a long way from the bedroom.

3 The father left the children alone for hours; that's so _____ .

4 She's very _____ ; she doesn't give me time to answer the questions.

5 She's terrified of heights, but she goes climbing. That seems _____ to me!

6 They asked me to pay for work they didn't do; that's so _____ .

7 The office is terribly _____ ; you can never find anything.

8 The plans were interesting but totally _____ ; much too expensive.

*go to **language reference** p.167*

how to ... learn English faster

Your English will improve more quickly if you can carry on learning out of class time. This lesson will give you ideas and strategies to help the process.

how long would it take?

Think! Decide how long each idea would take. You have one minute! Compare your answers with a partner.

		How long?
1	memorize 15 new irregular verbs and get them right	
2	look up five new words in a dictionary	
3	complete a page of your workbook	
4	write a letter in English to a friend	
5	read a one-page magazine article in English	
6	tell someone in English everything you did yesterday	

natural English
use of *take*
(9.4)

How long would it **take** (you) to do that exercise?
It would **take** (me) about half an hour.

Does it **take** (you) long to get there?
No, not very long.

Listen. Do you hear the words in brackets?
Practise the phrases.

grammar frequency adverbs and adverbial phrases

1   Put these words / phrases in the correct place on the line below.

occasionally /əˈkeɪʒənli/   rarely /ˈreəli/   almost always   quite often   hardly ever

never   sometimes   often   always

2   Look at the speech bubbles.

1   For each sentence, find one position where all the adverbs in **exercise 1** could go.

2   Which adverbs / phrases can go at the <u>beginning</u> of the sentences?

> I'm too tired to study in the evening.

> I have the opportunity to speak English out of class time.

> I do my English homework on time.

> I've been late for class because of the traffic.

3   Make the sentences true for you and tell a partner.

go to **language reference** *p.168*

English out of class time

1   Work with a partner. Which activities below can help you practise speaking, listening, reading, or writing?

1   see a film in English (with subtitles) at the cinema or on video

2   start up a conversation with some English-speaking tourists

3   look at English-language newspapers or magazines

4   follow the words of a song in English

5   use the Internet to find out about things that interest you

6   send and receive e-mails in English

7   go to an event in English in your town (a play, a talk)

8   watch a TV programme in English

9   join an English-speaking club

10   keep a diary in English

2   Tick ✓ the ones you've tried. Have you tried anything else?

3 **(9.5)** You're going to listen to Jackie, who teaches English in Italy, talking about how her students practise English out of class time. Listen to the beginning of the conversation. What does she mainly talk about: speaking, listening, reading, or writing?

4 Listen to the whole conversation. Tick ✓ any of the activities in **exercise 1** that Jackie mentions.

5 **Think!** Decide on two of the activities that Jackie describes that you'd like to try.

1 How can you do it?
2 What do you need?
3 Where can you do it?
4 Will you have any problems?
5 Do you need to do it with other learners?

6 Compare your ideas in small groups. In the next lesson, tell each other what you tried!

write a learning diary

Write your own diary for this week, like the one below. Write your plans for next week.

LEARNING DIARY

In class this week

1 I've learnt some vocabulary about _____ and we've practised conditional sentences.

2 We've talked about ...

3 We've listened to ...

Out of class this week

1 I've done some exercises from the workbook.

2 I've written an e-mail to a friend in America.

3 I've watched the news on CNN.

Out of class next week

1 I'm going to borrow an English video (a comedy).

2 I'm going to look at web pages on mountain bikes on the Internet.

🔊 **extended speaking**
Learn these phrases for later
I'm occasionally late for work.
I rarely look at my watch.
I hardly ever arrive on time.
Does it take you long to ...?

collect ideas

1 **Think!** Decide on your answer to <u>question 1 only</u> in the questionnaire.

2 Work in small groups. Find out other people's answers to question 1.

3 **Think!** Decide on your answers to questions 2 to 8.

ARE YOU A **SLAVE** TO TIME?

1 Do you think you are:
a always punctual?
b usually punctual but occasionally late?
c hardly ever on time?
Give examples and reasons.

2 Do you look at your watch or a clock:
a very often?
b occasionally?
c rarely?
Why (not)? In which situations?

3 If you have unpleasant jobs to do, do you:
a try to do them quickly?
b postpone them, and hope they go away?
c do them over a period of time?
Give examples.

4 If other people are late, does it make you angry?
a Yes, it annoys me.
b No, it doesn't bother me.
c Sometimes.
Give examples.

5 When you were a child (e.g. about 10 years old), did you:
a plan your own time?
b follow a timetable planned by your parents?
c plan your leisure activities, but follow your parents' timetable for homework and other jobs?
Can you remember examples?

6 If you had plans to go out with a friend on Sunday and your friend cancelled, would you:
a start to make new plans immediately?
b wait till Sunday and then make plans?
c do nothing on Sunday?
What are your reasons?

7 If your train was about to leave, would you run to catch it?
a Yes.
b No.
c Only if it was really urgent for you to catch it.
What are your reasons?

8 If you had to queue for more than two hours to get tickets for a concert or a sporting event, would you:
a queue happily?
b have doubts about queueing?
c decide not to wait?
Has this happened to you?

talk about the questionnaire

4 Work in small groups and talk about your answers.

natural English
asking about other people's answers

As you go through the questionnaire, you can use these phrases to introduce each question.

What did you put for number 1/the first question?
What have you got for number 2/the second question?

5 Look at the scores and the analysis on *p.145*. Do you agree with it? Talk about it in your group.

prepare your own questions

6 With a partner, think of <u>three</u> more questions about time to ask other people. Use these prompts, or your own ideas.

> **1** When you have to sit and wait a long time at the dentist's, do you:
>
> a _____
> _____
> b _____
> _____
> c _____
> _____

> **3** If the service is very slow in a café or restaurant, do you:
>
> a _____
> _____
> b _____
> _____
> c _____
> _____

> **2** If you had a free half hour before your English lesson, would you:
>
> a _____
> _____
> b _____
> _____
> c _____

> **4** If you had 26 weeks' holiday a year, would you:
>
> a _____
> _____
> b _____
> _____
> c _____
> _____

> **5** If you arrived ten minutes late for your English lesson, would you:
>
> a _____
> _____
> b _____
> _____
> c _____
> _____

7 Find a new partner. Ask them your questions. What do the answers tell you about your partner?

test yourself!

How well do you think you did the extended speaking? Mark the line.

0 ────────────────────── 10

From this unit, write down:

1 three ways of saying *approximately 6.00*.

2 the negative prefixes of these adjectives: ___ *convenient*, ___ *logical*, ___ *practical*, ___ *responsible*, ___ *efficient*, ___ *fair*, ___ *organized*.

3 the difference between these pairs: *postpone / cancel, meeting / date, on time / in time, pick sb up / drop sb*.

Complete the sentences. The meaning must stay the same.

1 I find traffic noise slightly irritating.
Traffic noise _____ .

2 I tidied the kitchen as quickly as possible.
I tidied the kitchen in _____ .

3 What time do you make it?
Have _____ ?

4 I don't mind if they arrive late.
It doesn't _____ .

Correct the errors.

1 If I'd earn a lot of money, I'd get a new car.

2 I can see better at football matches if I was taller.

3 I do often my homework on time.

4 We can go out this afternoon if the weather will be nice.

Look back at the unit contents on *p.103*. Tick ✓ the language you can use confidently.

three mothers

how to ... react to a joke

That's funny.

That's a great joke.

I don't get it.

That's awful.

I've heard it before.

do you get it?

in unit ten ...
tick ✓ when you know this

natural English

the whole ... ☐
generalizations (2) ☐
get + past participle (passive use) ☐
describing stereotypes ☐
invitations ☐
making and accepting excuses ☐

grammar

articles and determiners ☐
defining relative clauses ☐

vocabulary

parties ☐
describing character ☐
collocation ☐

wordbooster

reasons for being late ☐
suffixes ☐

with a partner ...

Who do you think get on best, and why?

a fathers and daughters   c mothers and daughters
b mothers and sons   d fathers and sons

joke time

Look at the pictures. The three mothers each have a grown-up son, and they're **boasting** about them. What do you think the first two women are saying?

 Listen and react to the joke. Did you get it?
Go to *p.36* of the listening booklet and listen again.

---

 the whole ... /həʊl/

I spent **the whole time** worrying. = all the time
We went round **the whole country**. = all the country
The whole thing was a disaster. = the complete situation

Say the phrases. Then answer the questions.

example   Did you drink one glass?   No, I drank the whole bottle.

1 Did you read the first chapter?
2 Did he just eat one biscuit?
3 Did she only see the beginning of the film?

---

parties

Circle the correct answer.

1 a party in your new home: house-warming / house-heating party
2 man who invites people to a meal or party: host / hostess
3 a person who goes to a party without being invited: housecrasher / gatecrasher
4 party where you wear unusual clothes to be a different character: fancy dress / funny dress party
5 a formal party after a wedding ceremony: wedding reception / banquet
6 a person who is invited to a party or meal: guest / visitor

reading those teenage years

lead-in

1 Think! Decide on your answers to these questions about teenagers.

1 How would you describe the looks, clothing, and attitude of the teenagers in the pictures?

2 What kind of teenager are / were you? (e.g. hard-working? rebellious?) Describe yourself in three adjectives.

3 What are / were your teenage friends like?

2 Compare your answers in small groups.

grammar articles and determiners

1 Put *the* in the gaps below where necessary.

1 ___ parents always want the best for their children.

2 Actually, ___ woman who rang me yesterday was Lucy's teacher.

3 ___ teenagers are often rude, but they don't usually mean it.

4 I'm sure that ___ girls grow up much quicker than they used to.

5 ___ men that I know all seem to do more cooking than their wives.

6 ___ kids in general spend too much time on their computers.

7 ___ life is difficult for ___ elderly people without transport.

8 I really like ___ teachers at my daughter's school.

2 Circle the correct forms to complete the rules.

1 When we talk about people or things in general, we use / don't use the definite article with uncountable or plural nouns.

2 When we talk about someone or something specific, we use / don't use the definite article.

go to **language reference** *p.169*

generalizations (2) 10.2

These ways of generalizing can be useful to help you sound more diplomatic.

I think parents **tend to** worry too much about their _____ .

On the whole, parents are stricter with their first child than _____ .

Listen and fill the gaps above.
Say the sentences.

Do you agree or disagree with the statements? Tell a partner.

3 Think! Complete these statements.

Teenagers tend to _____ .

On the whole, parents _____ .

4 Compare your ideas with a partner.

5 Correct the errors at the beginning of each statement.

1 Most of teenagers tend to go out in large groups.

2 Almost teenage boys are more interested in football than the opposite sex.

3 All of teenagers are allowed to stay out later at weekends.

4 Most the teenagers I know have parties for their friends at their family home.

5 Some of parents let their teenagers have a party at home and go out themselves.

6 The most teenagers don't imagine things can go wrong at their party.

go to **language reference** *p.169*

6 Look again at the statements in **exercise 5**. Make them true for your country and compare with a partner.

read on

1 Read the article with the glossary.

2 With a partner, decide what you think was the worst thing that happened.

3 At whose party did the following happen: Rochelle's, Zoe's, or Luke's?

1 Some uninvited guests arrived.
2 Some people got wet.
3 Something got stolen from the fridge.
4 A boy had to pay for what he had done.
5 The hostess felt very embarrassed.
6 Something got broken.

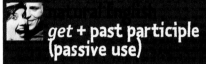

get + past participle (passive use)

This is a kind of passive structure used in informal English. It means that someone did something but you don't know who, often something unexpected or unplanned.

Several things **got stolen** at the party.
The glass door **got smashed**.
I don't know how that vase **got broken**.

Say the phrases. Make up sentences about another party, using *got stolen*, *got smashed*, and *got broken*.

it's your turn!

1 Talk about these questions in small groups.

1 What's your reaction to the article?
2 Do you agree with the advice at the end, or can you give any other advice?
3 Have you ever been to a party where something funny or terrible happened?

2 🔊 **10.3** Listen to two men talking about teenage parties they had. In A / B pairs, A remember story 1 and B remember story 2.

3 Tell your partner the story you memorized.

🎧 extended speaking

Learn these phrases for later
I think most women are ...
The men in my family are ...
On the whole, men are ...
Women tend to ...

The whole thing was a nightmare ...

Never again. That's the phrase that should be written in lipstick on the bathroom mirror of every parent who has ever let teenagers give a party at home. Yet every weekend, thousands of parents not only agree to let their teenage children have a party at home,
05 they also find themselves nodding happily and saying, 'Oh, well, if you're sure you want us to go out …'

This is what happened at ROCHELLE COHEN's 15th birthday party. Only now, 15 years later, can she and her father talk about it. Laughing about it may take another 15 years.

10 The house started to fill up with her friends, and then a group of gatecrashers arrived. She can recall the glass front door being smashed and some of her older friends taking the key to her father's very expensive car and driving round the city. But the worst part was when her father came home and discovered that 30 computer games were missing. He telephoned
15 the parents of all his daughter's friends. In the end, a boy from a very wealthy family brought them back.

'The whole thing was a **nightmare**,' says Rochelle. 'The party was bad enough, but to have my dad ringing everyone like that, I was so embarrassed.'

ZOE MARKS remembers a party she had. 'Someone filled the bath with
20 water, then added tomato sauce, and everyone jumped in. They then went down to the beach to go swimming, where someone stole most of their clothes. At six in the morning, their poor parents received a phone call, asking them to come and collect them.'

Many parents return home to find their houses emptied of everything except
25 the dog food. At the end of LUKE BARTON's party, his father (a policeman) came home to find some young guests had eaten a kilo packet of smoked salmon. He said he was going to test for **fingerprints** to find out who had opened the packet. The guilty boy admitted it immediately, and his parents were sent a bill.

30 So the advice to parents is – stay at home. Or prepare for a nightmare on your return.

glossary

Complete with words from the article.
a _____ (para 1) make-up women put on their mouth
b _____ (para 1) move your head up and down to say 'yes'
c _____ (para 3) break into small pieces
nightmare /'naɪtmeə/ like a bad dream; a horrible real experience
d _____ (para 6) responsible for doing something bad
fingerprint mark made by the lines on your fingers

vocabulary describing character

1 Think! What is the stereotype of politicians in your country? Do you agree with these opinions? Can you add other ideas?

a They're hard-working and caring /ˈkeərɪŋ/.

b They're mostly honest /ˈɒnɪst/ and tell the truth.

c I think they're all liars /ˈlaɪəz/ – and they're corrupt /kəˈrʌpt/ too.

d They're incredibly self-confident.

e They often make promises they don't keep.

f Some of them are extremely nice – too nice.

2 Say the phrases. Compare your ideas with a partner.

3 Complete the dialogues with the character adjectives from the box.

lazy	mature /məˈtʃʊə/	conventional /kənˈvenʃənl/
patient /ˈpeɪʃnt/	sensitive	loyal /ˈlɔɪəl/

1 **A** Sheila always thinks about other people's feelings.

   B Yes, I agree, she's very _____ .

2 **A** I think Dave is much more adult and grown up now.

   B Yes, he seems a lot more _____ these days.

3 **A** Judy doesn't get annoyed or try to rush people.

   B Yes, I find her very _____ .

4 **A** Mark stayed with the company even when they treated him badly.

   B Yes, I know, he's very _____ .

5 **A** My brother does absolutely nothing all day.

   B I know, he's incredibly _____ , isn't he?

6 **A** She never does anything unusual or unexpected; she's such a conformist.

   B Yes, I know, she's very _____ .

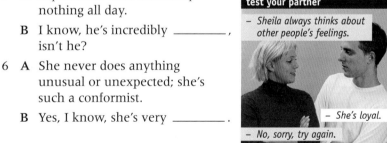

test your partner
- Sheila always thinks about other people's feelings.
- No, sorry, try again.
- She's loyal.

4 The opposite of 'lazy' is 'hard-working', but the other adjectives in **exercise 3** form opposites with prefixes. What are they?

lead-in

Think! What is your stereotype of the people listed below? Think of two or three ideas for each one. Then compare with a partner.

primary school teacher
rock star
football supporter
chat show host
university student
soldier

describing stereotypes

People often say that nurses are very caring.
Actors **are supposed** /səˈpəʊzd/ **to be** very emotional.
Teachers **are said to be** very hard-working.

Say the phrases.

listen to this

tune in

1 You're going to listen to three people describing their stereotypes of the people in **lead-in**. Before you listen, look at these extracts. Which people do you think they're describing?

   1 … they were on the whole very caring …

   2 … people assume that they're lazy …

   3 … they're only really interested in asking questions …

2 Listen to the three people. Were you right?

listen carefully

3 Listen to the whole conversations. Write T (true) or F (false).

   1 Marcella thinks primary teachers are gentle.

   2 She believes that all primary teachers are caring.

   3 Michael thinks most chat show hosts don't listen to their guests.

   4 He doesn't think there are any good chat show hosts.

   5 Gareth says that people think students are untidy.

   6 The students he knows are hard-working.

4 Do you agree with the speakers? Why / why not?

listening challenge

5 Listen to DeNica and Jonathan talking about rock stars. What do they think of them? Tell a partner. Listen again with the tapescript if you need to.

listening booklet *p.36 to p.39*

grammar defining relative clauses

1 Which words (*who, which, that*) can you put in the gaps?

   1 I think people _____ present chat shows well really listen to their guests.

   2 I don't like chat shows _____ only show you the good side of famous people.

2 Join the sentence halves using *who / that* or *which / that*.

1 I only watch TV programmes	who / that	sit next to me on the train.
2 I prefer stories	which / that	make a lot of noise.
3 I hate drivers		are all about love.
4 I give money to anyone		teach me something.
5 I don't understand people		asks me.
6 I often speak to passengers		they've given me.
7 I always thank people for presents		think the worst will always happen.
8 I don't mind neighbours		go very slowly.

3 Decide what kind of person said each sentence.

   example I only watch TV programmes which / that teach me something. = a serious person

4 In which sentence can you omit *that*, and why? (Notice the kind of word which follows *who / which / that*.)

go to **language reference** *p.170*

🔊 extended speaking

Learn these phrases for later

Men who are … often …

Men are said to be …

People that … have to …

They're more loyal / sensitive / hard-working.

wordbooster

reasons for being late

1 Choose the correct word in brackets.

1 I got home three hours late because I (lost / missed) the last bus.
2 I missed my appointment because my car (had / took) a puncture.
3 We were late because we (bumped / jumped) into an old friend in the supermarket.
4 'The train drivers are (in / on) strike again so I'm going to be late.'
5 'I'm so sorry, Mrs Robson. I got held (over / up) in traffic.'
6 I missed the wedding because my car broke (down / up) on the motorway.
7 My alarm clock didn't go (out / off) and I didn't wake up until 10.30.
8 'Sorry I'm late. I got off the bus at the wrong (stop / station).'

2 Work with a partner.

1 Which reasons for being late are most common among your family and friends?
2 When was the last time one of these happened to you? What happened?

suffixes

1 Complete the noun column and the correct suffix for each group.

+ness	+y / +ty	+ance / +ence	+ity

adjective	noun	adjective	noun
1	+ _____	3	+ _____
tolerant	_____	tidy	_____
ignorant	_____	lazy	_____
confident	_____	polite	_____
patient	_____	kind	_____
2	+ _____	4	+ _____
punctual	_____	honest	_____
similar	_____	modest	_____
stupid	_____	cruel	_____
mature	_____	loyal	_____

2 In which examples are there spelling changes? Circle them in a different colour.

go to **language reference** *p.170*

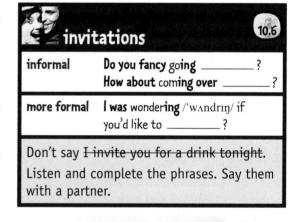
If you don't want to (or can't) do something, people may accept it more easily if you have a good excuse.

how about it?

1 Think! In these situations, would you tell the truth, or invent an excuse? Why?

a Someone suggests you go to a very expensive restaurant together, but you can't afford it.

b A friend invites you to dinner, and you know someone that you really dislike is also going to be there.

c You offer to go and see a sick friend this evening. Later, your brother offers you a ticket to see a fantastic concert tonight. What would you say to your friend?

2 Compare your ideas with a partner.

invitations		10.6
informal	**Do you fancy** going _____ ? **How about** coming over _____ ?	
more formal	**I was** wondering /ˈwʌndrɪŋ/ if you'd like to _____ ?	

Don't say ~~I invite you for a drink tonight~~.
Listen and complete the phrases. Say them with a partner.

3 With a partner, think of three more invitations for this weekend.

make excuses

excuses

vocabulary collocation

1 Complete the sentences using the words/phrases. Sometimes more than one answer is possible.

pick up	go and see	write	do
sort out	prepare	babysit	go to
see sb off	go away	deliver	give

1 _____ somebody a lift to the hospital
2 _____ for a friend
3 _____ a problem with my boss
4 _____ a friend from the airport
5 _____ clients /'klaɪənts/
6 _____ revision
7 _____ documents
8 _____ on business
9 _____ a presentation
10 _____ a rehearsal /rɪ'hɜːsl/
11 _____ at the airport
12 _____ an essay

2 Match all the phrases in **exercise 1** to these three groups. Some phrases can go in more than one column.

studying	work	free time

3 Which of these things do you do, and how often? Tell a partner.

making and accepting excuses

excuses	I'd love to, but (unfortunately) ...
	I'm afraid I can't.
	I've got to work tonight.
	Sorry, but I won't be able to, because ...
accepting excuses	Never mind.
	That's a pity/shame.
	Another time, maybe.

Memorize the phrases. Practise the dialogues with a partner.

1 Move around the class inviting people to do things and making/accepting excuses.

2 You're going to listen to a conversation between Alison and Max. They've arranged to meet for a drink but she's late. Think of three possible reasons.

3 **(10.7)** Listen to **part 1** of the conversation. With a partner, ask and answer the questions.

1 How many voices do you hear?
2 Why is she late?

4 Read the summary. Listen to **part 2**. Correct four factual errors.

> Alison invites Max to go to a dance at the Sheraton Hotel on Sunday evening. He'd like to go, but he's got a lot to do this weekend, because he has to prepare a presentation for 50 people for Monday, and he's busy on Sunday because he's going to his stepson's house.

it's your turn!

1 In A/B pairs, A turn to *p.145* and B to *p.147*.

2 Change roles. A turn to *p.147* and B turn to *p.145*.

3 Work in groups of three. Write invitations to the two other people in your group. They should accept one and refuse the other, with an excuse.

extended speaking

men and women

you're going to:

collect ideas
discuss a statement about men and women

extend the discussion
discuss more statements and add your own

summarize opinions
record your group's opinions and summarize them to the class

but first ...
Look back at the **extended speaking** boxes in this unit. You can use this language in the activity.

 collect ideas

1 **Think!** Look at the statement. Do you agree or disagree? Why / why not?

Men spend more time on the phone than women.

2 Compare your ideas with a partner.

3 (10.8) Listen to Julia and Jonathan. Who agrees with the statement?

4 Listen again. What reason does each one give?

 extend the discussion

5 **Think!** Read the statements. Decide whether you think they are completely true ✓✓, mostly true ✓, mostly false ✗, or definitely false ✗✗, and why.

	topics	statements	
1	**at home**	**Men** are much tidier than **women**.	☐
2	**character**	**Women** are much better liars than **men**.	☐
3	**health**	**Men** take more time off work than **women**.	☐
4	**friendship**	**Men** make more loyal friends than **women**.	☐
5	**social interaction**	**Men** interrupt more often than **women**.	☐
6	**driving**	**Women** drive more carefully than **men**.	☐
7			☐
8			☐

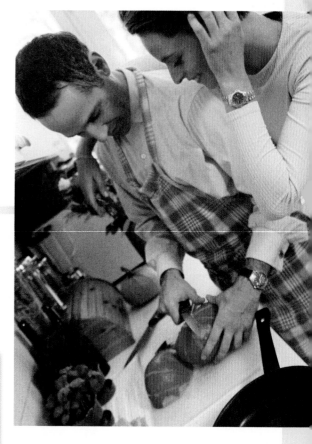

6 Work with a partner. Don't discuss the statements yet. Add two more topics and statements. Choose your own, or use these ideas.

love / relationships	shopping
attitudes to studying	manners
food / eating habits	careers
clothes and appearance	learning languages

7 Work in mixed groups of men and women, if possible. Discuss all the statements. Give examples and reasons.

language reminder
When you're agreeing with someone, say:
  I think you're right.
  Yes, I agree.
  You're absolutely right.
Don't say:
  ~~I'm agree with you.~~

test yourself!

How well do you think you did the extended speaking? Mark the line.

0   10

From this unit, write down:

1 five reasons for being late, e.g. *miss the bus / train*.

2 the nouns from these adjectives: *patient, honest, tidy, cruel, punctual, confident, mature*.

3 five character adjectives with a negative meaning, e.g. *disloyal*.

Complete the sentences. The meaning must stay the same.

1 I spent all afternoon working.
   I worked the _____ .

2 Someone smashed the window.
   The window _____ .

3 How about coming for a drink?
   Do _____ ?

4 Sorry, but I'm busy tonight.
   I'm _____ .

Correct the errors.

1 Most of students are very hard-working.

2 I can't understand people which speak fast.

3 Parents don't always understand the teenagers.

4 Nurses said to be very caring.

Look back at the unit contents on *p.115*. Tick ✓ the language you can use confidently.

summarize opinions

8 In your group, summarize your opinions in the table below. For example, if two people thought that 'Men are much tidier than women' was definitely true, write '2' in the first column; if three people thought it was definitely false, write '3' in the last column.

topics	✓✓	✓	✗	✗✗
1 at home	☐	☐	☐	☐
2 character	☐	☐	☐	☐
3 health	☐	☐	☐	☐
4 friendship	☐	☐	☐	☐
5 social interaction	☐	☐	☐	☐
6 driving	☐	☐	☐	☐

9 Choose one person in your group to summarize to the class.

1 Which statements caused most disagreement?

2 Which results surprise you?

3 What were your own topics and statements?

photo booth

life with Agrippine

in groups ...

When was the last time you used a photo booth?

Where was it, what were the photos for, and what were they like?

cartoon time

Read the cartoon. Why do Agrippine and her friend want to do the pictures again?

11.1 Listen and follow the cartoon. Then test your partner on the glossary words / phrases.

---

natural English
have (got) sth on, with sth on (= wearing)

He **hasn't got** anything **on**. = He isn't wearing any clothes.
I can't read it. I **haven't got** my glasses **on**.
That's her, the lady **with** the green hat **on**. = wearing the green hat

Say the phrases. With a partner think of four questions to ask the class.

examples How many people have got jeans on?
Who's got a black jacket on?

---

in unit eleven ...
tick ✓ when you know this

natural English
have (got) sth *on, with* sth *on* (= *wearing*) ☐
giving opinions about issues ☐
which clauses ☐
changing plans ☐
uses of *tell* ☐
sequencing ☐

grammar
passive forms ☐
look, look like, look as if ... ☐
modal verbs of deduction ☐

vocabulary
describing a picture ☐

wordbooster
word building ☐
time expressions ☐

---

glossary

horrendous /həˈrendəs/ horrible
with sth on / have sth on wearing sth
polo neck jumper with a high neck
you can say that again ☺ I completely agree with you
get changed put on different clothes

lead-in

1 **Think!** Look at the two photos and find five differences between them.

2 Check your ideas with a partner.

3 Say the words.

photograph /'fəʊtəgrɑːf/
photography /fə'tɒgrəfi/
photo /'fəʊtəʊ/

read on

1 Read the article with the glossary. Did you find **all** the differences between the two photos?

2 Answer the questions.

1 How were the picture editors able to change the photos?

2 Why are photos changed in newspapers?

3 Explain the meaning of these idiomatic phrases in the text.

a *the camera never lies* (line 01)

b *there's nothing wrong with making the grass a bit greener* (line 41)

natural English
giving opinions about issues

I **think it's OK to** make people look more attractive. ☺
I **don't see any problem if** newspapers change pictures.
I **don't think it's right to** take pictures of celebrities on holiday.

Say the sentences.

This is how easy it is to retouch history

People used to say that 'the camera never lies', but with modern computer software and digitized photographs, almost anyone can now change the content of a photograph.

Take the two photos above
05 as an example. With the aid of a computer program, the second man from the left was **removed** and the background

was darkened. That done, Robin
10 Cook (the man on the left-hand side) was moved closer to Tony Blair (the man in the middle). The ugly red plastic in the

Match the words with the definitions.

	glossary		
1	**remove** /rɪ'muːv/	a	make sth better
2	**replace**	b	be the right size or shape
3	**improve** /ɪm'pruːv/	c	put one thing in place of another
4	**fit** (v)	d	take sth out

foreground was also removed, and in its place we put a bottle of champagne. And finally, Gordon Brown (the man on the right). His serious face was **replaced** with a much happier smiling face, which was chosen from an electronic picture library. The picture editor could have just replaced the smile, but as the eyes were shut, it was decided to replace his whole head.

For years newspapers have used various techniques to **improve** the quality of their photographs, and have often moved people closer together to make them **fit** on the page of the paper. But now some editors feel that too many changes are being made. One former editor said: 'It's being untruthful with a picture, and we'd never agree to anyone telling a lie in words, so we shouldn't do it with pictures.' Another former editor agreed but took a slightly more relaxed view: 'There's nothing wrong with making the grass a bit greener, but if you start removing people because they aren't what you want, then where will it end?'

3 **Think!** Is it right to do these things?

a Change a photo of a famous person to make them look more / less attractive.

b Improve a photo in an advert to make the product look more attractive.

c Publish photos of politicians' children.

d Change a war photo to make it look more or less violent than it is.

4 Compare your ideas in groups.

grammar passive forms

1 Work with a partner. Look at lines 04 to 25 again and answer the questions.

1 Are we more interested in <u>who</u> changed the photos, or <u>what happened</u> to them?

2 Which verb form is used most? Underline six examples.

2 Complete the table. Say the passive sentences. How are the auxiliary verbs pronounced?

active form	passive form
We make phones and faxes here.	Phones and faxes _____ .
She's selling her old house.	Her old house _____ .
He sent the letter yesterday.	The letter _____ .
They've offered me the job.	I _____ .
He'll finish the report later.	The report _____ .

go to **language reference** *p.171*

3 (11.2) You're going to listen to someone describing a friend, Patric. Work with a partner.

1 Listen and tune in to get the general idea. Don't write anything.

2 Listen again and take notes. Write the key words only.

3 With a partner, try to write the text using your notes.

4 Listen again to improve your text.

5 Check your text with the tapescript in the **listening booklet** on *p.40*.

4 In A / B pairs, check your ideas. A read the text on *p.146* and B read the text on *p.148*.

5 Tell each other about your photos. Explain:

1 who's in the photos.

2 how your photo was changed.

3 why it was changed.

grammar *look, look like, look as if ...*

1 Work with a partner. Look at the photos on *p.146* and *p.148* again and decide who these sentences describe.

1 They all look cheerful.
2 They look suntanned and relaxed.
3 He looks like an army general.
4 They look like businessmen.
5 He looks as if he's going to pull a gun out of his pocket.
6 They look as if they're chatting.

2 Complete the rules.

There are three common phrases with the verb *look*.

1 *look* + _____
2 *look like* + _____
3 *look as if* + _____

3 Make three sentences about people in your class using the phrases. Don't write the name. Ask your partner to guess who your sentences are about.

go to **language reference** *p.172*

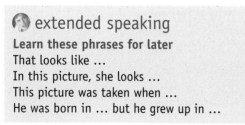

extended speaking

Learn these phrases for later
That looks like ...
In this picture, she looks ...
This picture was taken when ...
He was born in ... but he grew up in ...

wordbooster

word building

1 Find words in the tables that mean the following:
a feel sorry that you did or didn't do something
b a lot of money that a person has
c succeed in doing something through hard work and ability
d good feeling you have when you or those close to you do something well
e give up work, usually at 60 or 65
f choose someone to do a job by voting for them
g situation of having very little money
h something that you very much want to have or to do

verb	noun	adjective(s)	noun
retire /rɪˈtaɪə/	_____	_____	satisfaction
achieve /əˈtʃiːv/	_____	_____	success /səkˈses/
regret	_____	_____	politics /ˈpɒlətɪks/
believe (in)	_____	_____	pride
fail	_____	_____	fame /feɪm/
grow	_____	_____	wealth /welθ/
elect	_____	_____	ambition
solve	_____	_____	poverty

2 Complete the tables and mark the stress on each word.

test your partner
– *Retire – what's the noun?*
– *Retirement.*
– *That's right.*

time expressions

1 Is there a difference between the pairs of phrases? If so, what?

1 towards /təˈwɔːdz/ the end of the film | at the end of the film
2 next month | the following month
3 shortly after the wedding | soon after the wedding
4 during the war | throughout /θruːˈaʊt/ the war
5 last year | in the last year

2 Choose three sentence endings below. Complete them about yourself.

example __I was at school__ throughout the 1980s.

_____ throughout the 1980s.

_____ towards the end of the 1990s.

_____ in the last few years.

_____ during my lifetime.

listening

looking back over a lifetime

lead-in

Look at the photos. Who are they, and what are / were they famous for? Which person's autobiography would you most like to read?

listen to this

tune in

1 **(11.3)** You're going to listen to Elly, a 20-year-old student. Listen to the beginning of her story. What do you learn about:

– her birthplace?
– her family?
– her education?

listen carefully

2 Elly is imagining that she's now 70, and is inventing what happened in her life from now to age 70. What do you think goes in the gaps?

> After university she worked for ¹ _____ , but she soon realized that she wanted to become ² _____ , so she studied at ³ _____ for three years. While she was there, she met ⁴ _____ .
>
> In her thirties, she was offered ⁵ _____ ; it was very successful. Later she moved into ⁶ _____ .
>
> She changed direction completely in her mid-fifties, when she and her husband ⁷ _____ and went to live on ⁸ _____ .

3 Listen and complete the story.

listening challenge

4 **(11.4)** Listen to the end of Elly's autobiography. Answer the questions with a partner. Listen again with the tapescript if you need to.

1 Something unexpected happens in her life. What is it?
2 What does she think is her greatest achievement?

5 If you were Elly, what would you like / not like about your life?

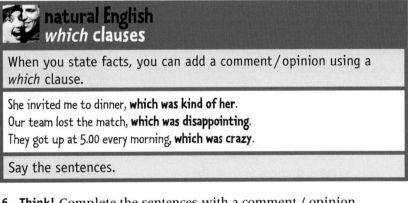

natural English
which clauses

When you state facts, you can add a comment / opinion using a *which* clause.

She invited me to dinner, **which was kind of her.**
Our team lost the match, **which was disappointing.**
They got up at 5.00 every morning, **which was crazy.**

Say the sentences.

6 **Think!** Complete the sentences with a comment / opinion.

1 I missed the last train home, which _____ .
2 All of our class passed their exams, which _____ .
3 My partner was late for class, which _____ .
4 Unfortunately, his trousers fell down, which _____ .

7 Compare your sentences with a partner.

listening booklet *p.40 and p.41 for tapescripts and exercises*

it's your turn!

1 Think! Imagine you're either 50 or 70 years old. Think about what has already happened in your life, and invent what happens after now. Use some of the prompts below to help you.

place of birth

marriage / children

family

career / change of career

education

major unexpected event in your life

military service (army, navy, air force)

after retirement

first job

greatest achievement

changing plans

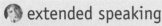

natural English
changing plans   11.5

I **was hoping to** work in television, **but in the end**
_____.

I **was planning to** travel a lot, **but I ended up**
_____.

Listen and complete the sentences.
Practise saying them.

With a partner, invent another sentence about education or marriage.

2 Work with a partner. Tell them about your real and invented life. Your partner should listen, and ask questions at the end.

examples

What was your greatest achievement?

Is there anything you regret?

3 Write a few sentences to describe part of your invented life. Look again at the story in **listen carefully**, and use it as a model.

extended speaking
Learn these phrases for later
After university, he joined ...
While he was there, he ...
Shortly after that, he moved to ...
She went to ..., which was very interesting.

how to ...
talk about a picture

artistic tastes

1 Think! What kind of paintings do you like?

  a old, modern, or both?

  b landscape (= countryside) or portraits (= people), or both?

  c realistic or abstract, or both?

  d any particular artists?

2 Compare your preferences with a partner.

vocabulary describing a picture

1 Match each phrase with a number in painting A.

  In the foreground there's a table / there are ...

  In the background you can see ...

  The man **on the (far)** left-hand side looks ...
              right-hand side is ...

  In the middle there's / there are ...

  In the top left-hand **corner,** you can just see ... (= you can see,
     bottom right-hand   but it's not easy)

2 Practise saying the phrases in **bold**.

3 Use the phrases to describe the picture.

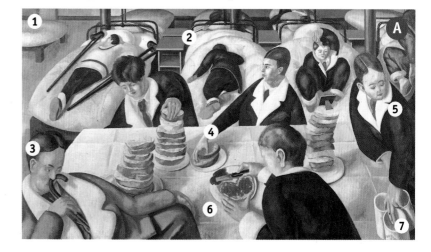

grammar modal verbs of deduction

1 These sentences refer to painting A. Match a and b with c or d.

1 a It's in a hospital.

    b It must be in a hospital.

   ···· c I'm not 100% sure, but it's the most logical explanation.

   ···· d I know for certain it's a hospital.

2 a The man on the bed on the left is sleeping.

    b The man on the bed on the left could be sleeping.

   ···· c I know he's sleeping.

   ···· d I think it's possible that he's sleeping.

3 a He might have a broken leg.

    b He must have a broken leg.

   ···· c It's possible that he has a broken leg.

   ···· d I'm 90% sure he has a broken leg.

4 a It isn't a 21st century painting.

    b It can't be a 21st century painting.

   ···· c I don't think it's possible that it is.

   ···· d I know for sure that it isn't.

go to **language reference** *p.172*

2 Which sentence in each pair do you think is true about painting A? Say them with a partner.

3 Make two more deductions. Use *must*, *might / could*, or *can't*.

4 Do you like painting A? Why / why not? Tell your partner.

natural English
uses of *tell*

You can't tell what's happening in the picture. It's wartime. **You can tell by** the clothes.
   = understand / recognize

It's hard to tell how old he is.
   = it's difficult to know / say for certain

Say the phrases.

5 Look at painting B. With a partner, answer the questions using *must*, *might / could*, or *can't*.

1 Who are the two old people? What are they doing?

2 Who's the little girl? What's she doing?

3 What's the relationship between the other people?

4 Is it in a town, a village, or the countryside?

5 What time of year is it?

6 What period is the painting?

7 Is it by the same artist as painting A?

6 What do you think of painting B?

it's your turn!

1 **Think!** In A / B pairs, A look at the painting on *p.171* and B on *p.173*. Prepare to:

a say where different things are in the painting.

b describe people / things.

c make deductions about the people / things / the place.

2 Work with a partner.

1 Describe your painting.

2 Which painting do you like most?

3 Do you think they are by the same artist?

extended speaking

Learn these phrases for later
In the foreground, there's a ...
In the bottom right-hand corner, I can see ...
This could / must be ...
I can't tell what's happening.

extended speaking

a life in pictures

you're going to:

collect ideas
describe and
sequence a set of
photos from a
person's life

develop the story
read some
information, imagine
the person's
biography, and tell
your story to
somebody else

find out the facts
hear the real story of
the person's life

but first ...
Look back at the
extended speaking
boxes in this unit.
You can use this
language in the
activity.

 collect ideas

1 **Think!** Look at the photos.
   1 What can you see in each one?
   2 Which person is the central character
     in the life story?
   3 Who could the other people be?
   4 What order do you think the photos
     should go in chronologically?

 natural English
sequencing

Which one do you think comes first?
This one could be the earliest / the most recent.
This one must come before that one.

Say the phrases.

2 Work with a partner.
   1 Agree who the central character is.
   2 Take it in turns to describe the photos.
   3 Discuss the order of the photos.

test yourself!

How well do you think you did the extended speaking? Mark the line.

0 ————————————————— 10

From this unit:

1 complete the structures: *She looks + _____ , He looks like + _____ , They look as if + _____ .*

2 write the nouns formed from these verbs: *believe, fail, succeed, grow, elect, achieve.*

3 mark the stress on these words: *satisfactory, political, success, achievement, ambitious, poverty.*

Complete the sentences. The meaning must stay the same.

1 I'm sure he knows them.
He must _____ .

2 Someone stole her bike.
Her bike _____ .

3 I'm sure he's not Spanish.
He _____ .

4 I think it's OK for papers to change stories.
I don't see _____ .

Correct the errors.

1 The books was been sent.

2 I saw him the last year.

3 The man at the left of the photo.

4 She helped me, which it was kind of her.

Look back at the unit contents on *p.125.* Tick ✓ the language you can use confidently.

develop the story

3 With your partner, use the photos to try to guess the story of the man's life.

example We think this man was probably born around 1920, and his family …

4 In A / B pairs, A read the information on *p.145* and B read the information on *p.149.*

5 Tell each other your story with the new information. What differences are there between your stories? Tell the class.

find out the facts

6 Listen to the story of the man's life. What new information do you hear about him? Compare with a partner.

7 Listen again with the tapescript on *p.40* of the **listening booklet.**

the gold watch

brand new (adj) completely new

show sth off show people sth you are proud of, to impress them

tear /teə/ **sth off** remove sth violently

cost a fortune cost a lot of money

disaster /dɪˈzɑːstə/ unexpected bad event

sleeve part of shirt that covers your arm

how to ... react to a joke

That's very funny.

Oh no!

That's horrible.

I don't get it.

That's a good one.

do you get it?

with a partner ...

If money were no object, which make or brand of these products would you buy?

car	watch	luggage
computer	trainers / shoes	perfume / aftershave

joke time

Look at the pictures. What's happening in each one? What's going to happen next?

 12.1 Listen to the joke. Did you get it?
Go to *p.42* of the listening booklet and listen again.

---

natural English
What a ...!

What a disaster!　**What a** nightmare!　**What a** terrible thing to happen!

Say the phrases. Respond to situations 1 to 3 with a partner.

1　Your national football team lost the World Cup final.
2　Someone stole all your money when you were on holiday.
3　Your new neighbours have loud parties every night.

---

driving

Match 1 to 5 with a to e.

1　Unfortunately, I **reversed**
2　The car **overtook**
3　I looked round, then **pulled out**
4　I managed to **park**
5　I **slowed down**

a　from the side of the road.
b　into a tree and damaged the car.
c　between the wall and the gate.
d　to keep to the speed limit.
e　the lorry in front.

test your partner
– The car overtook ...
– ... the lorry in front.
– Yes, that's right.

---

in unit twelve ...
tick ✓ when you know this

natural English
What a ...! ☐
realize, remember, find out ☐
direct speech in narrative ☐
numbers in phrases ☐
actually ☐
asking for clarification ☐

grammar
past perfect simple ☐
plural nouns ☐

vocabulary
driving ☐
money ☐

wordbooster
shopping ☐
phrasal verbs with *back* ☐

listening tell me what happened

lead-in

Look at the warning. Think of three situations where someone might say 'Be more careful!'.

BE MORE CAREFUL!

listen to this

tune in

1 **12.2** You're going to listen to Sam telling a true story. Listen to the beginning of his story and tune in to the voices and speed. Work with a partner and answer the questions.

  1 Where did Sam go?

  2 What was it like?

  3 What did he do afterwards?

listen carefully

2 Listen to the whole story. Why was Sam a bit angry about the warning he received?

3 Read the sentences and correct any factual errors.

  1 When Sam arrived home he still had his wallet.

  2 He thought he could have dropped the wallet on the way home.

  3 His wallet contained his name, address, and phone number.

  4 The man rang two weeks later.

  5 He said, 'I'll bring the wallet to your house'.

  6 When Sam got his wallet back, everything was there.

listening booklet *p.42 and p.43 for tapescript and exercise*

grammar past perfect simple

1 Choose the correct ending.

  1 Sam had a good meal, paid for it, and …

    a came home.   b had come home.

  2 When Sam got home …

    a he lost his wallet.   b he realized he'd lost his wallet.

  3 The man sent the wallet back. Sam opened it; the man …

    a put a note in it.   b had put a note in it.

2 Two of the correct sentences above are in the past perfect simple.

  1 How do you form it?

  2 Why is it used?

3 Choose the correct form in each sentence. In one sentence, both are possible.

1 It was only when I was leaving the station that I remembered I left / 'd left my jacket on the train.

2 They had / 'd had a very long break when I arrived, so we were able to start the meeting immediately.

3 She decided / 'd decided to move before they offered her the job.

4 I didn't phone at a good time, because Sonia had / was having a bath, and Michael went / had gone to bed.

5 I locked / 'd locked my wallet in the cupboard and went out.

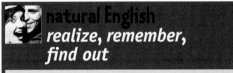

natural English (12.3)
realize, remember, find out

The past perfect is often used after the verbs *realize*, *remember*, and *find out*. Time markers, e.g. *suddenly, later, before*, and *already* are very common here.

I **suddenly remembered** (that) I'd left the gas on.
She **realized** (that) she'd met him **before**.
I **found out later** (that) he'd been in prison.
When the film started I **realized** (that) I'd **already** seen it.

Listen. Do you hear the words in brackets? Say the sentences without *that* and using the contractions (*'d*).

go to **language reference** *p.173*

listening challenge

(12.4) You're going to listen to Sally telling a story about how she was locked out of her house. What part did these people play in the story?

– Sally's husband
– her daughter
– the taxi driver

Listen again with the tapescript on *p.42* of the **listening booklet** if you need to.

story-telling

natural English
direct speech in narrative

It's very common in conversation to use direct speech when telling a story. It brings the story to life and makes it more dramatic.

... so I said, '**Look, I'm locked out, I don't know what to do**'.
... and he said, '**Well! What's the matter with you?**' I was so angry I just ...

1 You can also bring a story to life with interesting details. Read the text. With a partner, invent answers to the questions.

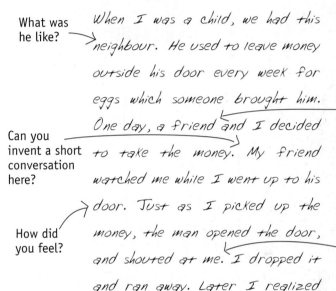

What was he like? → When I was a child, we had this neighbour. He used to leave money outside his door every week for eggs which someone brought him. One day, a friend and I decided to take the money. My friend watched me while I went up to his door. Just as I picked up the money, the man opened the door, and shouted at me. I dropped it and ran away. Later I realized I'd also dropped my school book with my name and address in it ...

Can you invent a short conversation here?

How did you feel?

What can you add about this friend?

What did he say? What did he sound like?

What happened afterwards? Invent your own ending.

2 Practise telling the story including your new information.

example When I was a child, we had this neighbour. He was a really horrible old man who didn't like children. He used to …

3 Tell your story to a new partner. What are the differences?

 extended speaking
Learn these phrases for later
I realized I'd …   I found out later he'd …
I hadn't … before.   Then he said, 'Why haven't you …?'

reading
attitudes to money

vocabulary money

1 Look at pictures 1 to 5. What are they?

2 Move around the class asking and answering questions.

	Find someone who ...	name
1	has ever lost their wallet / purse.	
2	doesn't like using cashpoints.	
3	keeps money in an unusual place.	
4	has or would like to have a safe.	
5	has spent too much this week.	
6	is saving up for something.	

3 Match the verbs with phrases in blue. Use each verb / phrase once only. Read your sentences to a partner.

example borrow £100 from someone until tomorrow

borrow   £10 in the street   **find**   £150 on clothes

£2,000 from a relative who's died   **lend**   a £50 phone bill   **invest**

lose   £100 from someone until tomorrow   **win**   your wallet with a £50 note in it

someone £100 to buy a CD player   **spend**   £40 in overtime this week   **pay**

inherit   £3,000 in a new company   **earn**   a £2,000 prize

4 Complete the table using the information above. Use the past simple. Is the person 'in credit' (+) or 'in the red' (-) at the end?

money coming in	+	money going out	-
borrowed	£100	spent	£150

Adrian

Claire

Mary

---

natural English
numbers in phrases

Numbers can form adjectives before a noun. Notice they are <u>singular</u> in form.

a **ten-cent** coin
a **ten-pound** note   NOT ~~a ten pounds note~~
a **five-pound** phone card
a **two-thousand-dollar** reward

Say the phrases.
What's in your bag or wallet? Tell a partner.

read on

1 You're going to read some parents' views on pocket money. How do you think these sentences from the article continue?

1 (My 13-year-old and 10-year-old) generally spend it on ...

2 (My son Michael) will get £1 a week, £1.50 if he ...

3 I opened bank accounts for them, so that they ...

2 Compare with a partner.

3 Read the article. How do the sentences in **exercise 1** end?

How much pocket money should you give?

ADRIAN BUTLER
father of 13-year-old Christine and 10-year-old Joseph

My kids each get £5 a week from their grandad. That's the only money they get; they generally spend it on sweets or save it. When Christine wanted to buy a CD a few weeks
05 ago, she saved £10 and borrowed £4 from us, which she paid back over the next two weeks. The children are very good, and they love checking their purses. They're always thrilled to be spending their own money, and in
10 the last year, they've become more aware of what to spend it on. At Christmas, they each drew out £10 from their bank accounts, and went shopping; they bought me a garlic sausage!

CLAIRE SCOTT
mother of Michael, 8, Peter, 6, Thomas, 4, and baby Edward

15 None of my children get any pocket money yet, although we're shortly going to start with Michael. He'll get £1 a week, £1.50 if he keeps his room tidy. We haven't given him pocket money until now, because I think if
20 they're too young, they just tend to spend money on **rubbish** – they just rush out and go mad. If we go to a **funfair**, I'll give them a small amount each to spend on whatever they want, but when it's gone, that's it. They also
25 get money on their birthdays and when people visit, so they have something to save up in their piggy banks.

MARY CARTER
mother of two daughters aged 20 and 28

I started mine on pocket money when they were around ten. I opened bank accounts for
30 them so that they could learn to save, and we always gave them money every month so they could learn to **budget**. When they were ten, they got around £20 a month, and more as they got older. You have to **bear in mind** that
35 a night out with friends is easily going to cost £12 or £15 these days; my 20-year-old currently gets £80 a month. But we always help out if there's something special they need that they can't afford.

---

glossary

rubbish /ˈrʌbɪʃ/ things of poor quality
funfair /ˈfʌnfeə/ amusement park
budget (v) /ˈbʌdʒɪt/ plan and control how much to spend
bear in mind /maɪnd/ remember or consider

---

4 Read the article again. Which parent:
  a thinks little children waste money?
  b doesn't give their children any money?
  c wants to teach their children to use money sensibly?
  d at the moment, only gives their children money for special occasions?
  e has lent money to their children when they need it?
  f understands that life is expensive for children these days?

5 Which ideas in the article do you agree / disagree with most? Tell a partner.

it's your turn!

1 **Think!** Choose A or B. You're going to speak for one minute. Plan what to say.

A READ THIS IF YOU'RE A PARENT
1 Do / will you give your children pocket money? If so, how much? At what age?
2 Do you teach your children about money?
3 Do / will you pay your children if they do little jobs around the house?
4 Does / will it worry you how they spend their pocket money?

B READ THIS IF YOU'RE NOT A PARENT
1 Did your parents give you pocket money? If so, at what age and how much?
2 Did you have to work for pocket money as a child?
3 What did you spend your money on?
4 Did you save money to buy things?
5 Did you get money as a present?

2 Work in small groups. Take it in turns to speak. Think of questions to ask each other.

🔊 **extended speaking**
Learn these phrases for later
I spent $40 on it.
I'd lost my wallet / purse.
I couldn't really afford it.
I'd saved up for ages.

wordbooster

shopping

1 Complete the sentences with these words. Compare with a partner.

a sale / the sales	refund (n) /'ri:fʌnd/	receipt /rɪ'si:t/	exchange
overcharge	deposit /dɪ'pɒzɪt/	bargain /'bɑːgɪn/	

1 Do you normally keep the _____ for things you buy? If so, why?

2 Do you often buy things in _____ ? What is the best _____ you've ever found?

3 If you go back to a shop because you aren't satisfied with something you bought, is it generally easy to _____ it for something else?

4 Is it common for shop assistants to _____ people by mistake?

5 If you take something back, are there shops where it is difficult to get a _____ ? Have you ever asked for one? What happened?

6 When you buy something, do you ever have to pay a _____ ?

2 Ask and answer the questions in groups.

phrasal verbs with *back*

1 Replace the words in bold with a phrasal verb. Make any necessary changes in word order.

ask for sth back
take sth back
send sth back
get sth back

back

come back
go back
give (sb) sth back
pay sth / sb back

1 I **returned** to the shop and spoke to the manager.
2 She **returned** the dress the following day.
3 They said they wanted to **return** the radio to the manufacturer.
4 Fortunately he **returned** my money when he saw the hole in the shirt.
5 I lent him some money, and he **returned** it the following week.
6 He went shopping but **returned** with nothing.

2 Look at the diagram again. In which examples can you separate the verb and *back*?

go to **language reference** *p.173*

right thing in a shop

When you're shopping, there are certain predictable routines. You can prepare for these situations by learning set phrases and structures.

grammar plural nouns

1 Match the words and the pictures.

gloves /glʌvz/   knickers /'nɪkəz/
slippers /'slɪpəz/   boots /buːts/
trousers /'traʊzəz/ shorts /ʃɔːts/
tights /taɪts/   sunglasses /'sʌnglɑːsɪz/
jeans /dʒiːnz/   (under)pants /'ʌndəpænts/
socks /sɒks/   pyjamas /pə'dʒɑːməz/

2 Ask and answer with a partner.

1 Which clothes in the pictures do you buy most often? Which do you like / not enjoy buying?

2 Do you often go shopping for clothes?

3 How long does it usually take you to find what you want?

4 Do you go alone or with someone else?

5 Do you buy clothes on the Internet? If not, would you like to? Why / why not?

3 The nouns in **exercise 1** end in -s. How many can also be written without -s and keep the same meaning?

go to **language reference** *p.174*

4 Correct the errors. More than one answer may be possible.

1 I've got a new sunglasses.

2 He bought three trousers.

3 This short is too small.

4 Have you got a jeans like this in size 14?

5 Where is my underpants?

6 His clothes doesn't look very fashionable.

in a clothes shop

1 Imagine you're shopping for clothes. With a partner, answer the questionnaire.

... say the right thing

1 You are looking at the clothes. The shop assistant comes up to you. What does he / she ask you?

> Do you need any help?

2 You don't need any help. Complete this answer.

> No, thanks, I'm ...

3 Later on, you find a jumper you like, and you want to see what it looks like on you. What do you ask?

4 In fact, it's the wrong size. What do you say?

5 The shop assistant offers you a different size, but you just don't think it looks right on you. How can you say this?

6 You find one you like, eventually, and you decide to buy it. What do you say?

7 You buy a pair of gloves which you are going to give someone for their birthday. What could you ask the shop assistant to do?

2 Listen to a woman in a clothes shop. Tick ✓ the phrases you wrote in **exercise 1** if you hear them.

3 Listen again. Write down other phrases used in **exercise 1**.

natural English
actually

You can use *actually* in spoken English when something is the opposite of what people think or when you want to say *no*.

He looks old, but **actually** he's only 32.

A Could I borrow your car?   **B** **Actually**, I need it today, sorry.

Be careful. *Actually* does <u>not</u> mean *at the moment* in English. Say the phrases.

go to **listening booklet** *p.42 and p.43*

it's your turn!

Work in groups of three, A, B, and C. A Look at the role card on *p.145*, and B and C look at the role card on *p.147*.

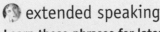 **extended speaking**

Learn these phrases for later

I tried it on.
They didn't fit me.

I bought a pair of gloves / pyjamas, etc.
It looked expensive, but actually ...

extended speaking

you're going to:

collect ideas
listen to a true story about shopping

prepare your story
think of a shopping experience and plan your story

tell your story
exchange stories with different partners

write your story
look at another shopping story from a magazine and write your own

but first ...
Look back at the **extended speaking** boxes in this unit. You can use this language in the activity.

collect ideas

1   Look at these shopping experiences. Which are positive (+) and which are negative (−)?

☐ You buy something which doesn't suit you.

☐ You find a bargain in a sale.

☐ You get overcharged.

☐ You take something back to a shop and get a full refund.

2   With a partner, think of one more positive thing and one more negative thing.

3   **12.6** Listen to **part 1** of Elspeth's true story. Answer questions 2 to 5 in the table.

4   Listen to **part 2**. Answer questions 6 and 7.

STORY FRAMEWORK	ELSPETH'S STORY
1 Where did it happen?	*We don't know*
2 When did it happen?	
3 What did the person want to buy, and why?	
4 What was the problem?	
5 How was it solved?	
6 Did anything unexpected happen at the end?	
7 What was the ending like? Was it positive, negative, funny, sad?	

prepare your story

5 **Think!** You're going to tell a partner about a good or bad shopping experience. Read the checklist.

- Use the questions in the framework to help organize your story.
- Use a dictionary or ask your teacher to help you with new words.
- Make notes, but don't write the full story.
- When you've finished, practise telling the story to yourself. This will help your confidence.

 tell your story

6 Work with a partner. Tell each other your stories. At the end, make sure you understand each other's stories. Use the phrases in the **natural English** box if necessary.

 natural English
asking for clarification

I didn't understand the bit about …
Could you explain the bit about … again?
I'm sorry but I didn't understand what / why / when / how …

7 You're now going to tell your partner's story. Tell it as if it's your <u>own</u> story. You may need to make small changes to sound realistic. Your partner should correct any factual mistakes you make.

8 Work with a <u>new</u> partner. Tell the two stories, without saying which one is yours. Your new partner can ask you questions. At the end, they have to decide which was your story, and why.

 write your story

9 Read this shopping story from a magazine. Answer questions 1 to 7 in the story framework.

• •

it happened to me …

On the last day of my holiday in the Bahamas, I bought a beautiful pair of shoes. They were quite expensive, but I decided they would be a nice souvenir of my holiday. I got back to my hotel in the evening and immediately wanted to try them on. When I took them out of the box, I realized that they had given me two left shoes! I ran back to the shop, just in case there was somebody there, but of course, it was closed. I flew home the next day with a useless pair of shoes.

10 Write your own story for the magazine, using the framework. Add more details to it. Show it to the partner you worked with and ask if they can identify the extra details.

---

test yourself!

How well do you think you did the extended speaking? Mark the line.

0 _____ 10

From this unit, write down:

1 six plural nouns which always end in -s, e.g. *trousers*.

2 six phrasal verbs with *back*.

3 six things you can do with money, e.g. *spend it*.

Complete the sentences. The meaning must stay the same.

1 John left the house. I arrived ten minutes later.
When I arrived _____ .

2 Where's the changing room?
Where can I _____ ?

3 It's the wrong size.
It doesn't _____ .

4 I got my money back.
I got a _____ .

Correct the errors.

1 I suddenly realized where I met him.

2 A ten-pounds note.

3 He spent the money for the car.

4 Oh no! What disaster!

Look back at the unit contents on *p.135*. Tick ✓ the language you can use confidently.

pairwork

one

how to ...
keep a conversation going

student A Complete the sentences.

I've just bought a new _____ .

We're going to spend two weeks in _____ .

They're building a _____ next to my home.

I've won a _____ .

In A / B pairs, take it in turns to read out your sentences and respond with interest.

two

extended speaking

student A You're the manager of a holiday complex. Listen to the tourist's problem, express sympathy, and ask any necessary questions. Offer to do something about it and say when you will do it.

four

extended speaking

student A You are one of the speakers who could give a talk on the course. One of the students is going to phone you and invite you to give your talk. You're very happy to be invited. Before you begin, plan your questions. You want to find out:

- date and place of the talk.
- the time of the talk, and how long it will be.
- the audience (who are they? how many people? what is their level of English?).
- is there a fee for the talk?
- is there anything else you need to know?
- give them your e-mail address (write it here) _____

five

how to ...
explain what to do

student A You're the owner of a coffee bar and you're giving the following instructions to a new member of staff.

- The soft drinks have to be very cold, and check the fridge is full.
- Don't let people leave the coffee bar without paying. Keep an eye on anyone sitting near the door.
- Ask people if they want anything to eat (this will be good for business).
- *your own idea* _____

six

how to ...
enquire about a course

student A You're the receptionist at a college. Your college has two courses in Travel and Tourism:

- a one-month course called 'Introduction to Tourism'
- a one-year course with a professional qualification called 'Diploma in Travel and Tourism'

Before you begin, fill the gaps below.

name of your college	
one-year course begins	
and ends	
full time course of	*hours per week*
cost of course is	
entry requirements	
number of students in class	
how to enrol	

Begin the phone conversation like this:

Hello, _____ College, how can I help you?

eight

how to ...
be a good guest

student A You're a student on a visit to Britain and you arrived at your landlord / landlady's home an hour ago. Before you begin, plan what you're going to say. You have three things to talk about:

1 You've spilt some juice on the carpet in your room. Say sorry!

2 You'd like to phone your family to tell them that you've arrived safely. Ask the landlord / landlady if you can use their phone.

3 You need to buy one or two things that you forgot to bring, e.g. toothpaste, a notebook. Ask your landlady / landlord where you can buy them locally.

You begin the conversation.

nine

extended speaking

SCORES

1	a	5	b	3	c	1	**5**	a	5	b	1	c	3
2	a	5	b	3	c	1	**6**	a	5	b	3	c	1
3	a	3	b	1	c	5	**7**	a	5	b	1	c	3
4	a	5	b	1	c	3	**8**	a	1	b	3	c	5

ANALYSIS

8 – 13
Time is a big problem for you. You're not very good at using your time well, and probably not very organized.

14 – 19
Time is a bit of a problem. You need to organize your time more efficiently.

20 – 25
This is an average score. You're quite relaxed, but still manage to do most things on time. You don't try to do too much, and this doesn't worry you.

26 – 31
You certainly know how to manage time, and you're very organized. Other people are surprised at how much you can do without stress. You may need to relax a bit more.

OVER 32
You're very productive, but this causes you anxiety, and sometimes you try to do too much. You're always racing against time, and find it very difficult to relax.

ten

how to ...
make excuses

student A You arrive at a coffee bar to meet a friend. You're 30 minutes late. Before you begin the conversation:

– think of one or two reasons why you are late.

– you're going to invite your friend to do something next Saturday; decide what it is, where, what time.

Begin the conversation like this:

Oh, hello, I'm really sorry I'm late …

eleven

extended speaking

student A Read this information and decide how to include it in the story of the man's life.

1 He went to Eton, which is a famous public school in England.

 public school (GB) a private school for pupils between the ages of 13 and 18, whose parents pay for their education

2 In 1956, he decided to stand for Parliament as a Liberal MP. He did well, but didn't win the election.

twelve

how to ...
say the right thing

student A You're an assistant in a clothes shop. You should try hard to sell the clothes in your shop. Try to persuade the customers to buy more things, e.g. if they buy a shirt, try to sell them a tie as well.

pairwork

reading
the camera never lies

text A

THE COMRADE WHO DISAPPEARED

The original photo below shows four men with Stalin in the middle. Later, however, the man on the right was removed. His name was Nikolai Yezhov, head of the **notorious** secret police from 1936 to 1938, who eventually lost favour and was later **executed** in 1940. At that time, it was common for certain characters to be removed from photographs, as it was all part of a **policy** to emphasize Stalin's importance.

glossary
notorious /nəʊˈtɔːrɪəs/ famous for something bad
be executed be killed as punishment for a 'serious' crime
policy plans that an organization has chosen to follow

one

how to ...
keep a conversation going

student B Complete the sentences.

I had to spend last night _____ .
My brother's found _____ .
I've just got a job as a _____ .
We're going to see _____ .

In A / B pairs, take it in turns to read out your sentences and respond with interest.

two

extended speaking

student B You're a tourist staying in a holiday complex. You're having problems with, e.g. the television, washing machine, or the air conditioning in your apartment / villa. Decide what the problem is, and think of a short story to explain what's happened.

six

how to ...
enquire about a course

student B You're interested in doing a course in Travel and Tourism, and you want to get a professional qualification. You've heard that there's a one-year course at your local college.

Before you begin, plan your questions. Here are three things you want to know:

– the course dates
– the number of hours per week
– the entry requirements

Think of three more things you want to know.

_____
_____
_____

eight

how to ...
be a good guest

student B You're a landlord / landlady and your visiting student arrived an hour ago. They have some things they want to talk to you about. Look at this information before you begin.

1   Guests often want to use your phone to call abroad, and you're a bit worried about this. You're quite happy for them to use the phone for local calls. You'll let them phone abroad once.

2   Your guest wants to go out and buy some things locally. Give them some simple directions and advice.

3   Tell them what time you eat in the evenings. (If the guest doesn't want to eat with you one evening, you need to know in the morning.)

ten

how to ...
make excuses

student B You're waiting in a coffee bar for a friend who's now 30 minutes late. Before you begin the conversation, read this information:

–   you are busy on Saturday during the day and the evening – decide what you're doing.

–   be ready to make some excuses when your friend invites you out. You could suggest a different day, or invite your friend to do something (plan what it might be).

eleven

how to ...
talk about a picture

twelve

how to ...
say the right thing

students B and C You're customers in a clothes shop. Both of you are looking for something new to wear.

–   Choose something and decide what colour, style, and size you want.

–   Ask the shop assistant if you can try it on.

–   Give each other advice on what to buy.

–   If necessary, ask for a different size, colour, etc.

–   Decide if you're going to buy it and pay.

pairwork

five

how to ...
explain what to do

student B You're a new member of staff in a coffee bar and the owner is going to give you instructions. Listen and ask about anything you don't understand.

- Ask when people have to pay – when they order, or when they are leaving?
- Ask if you can help yourself to food and drinks.
- *your own idea* _____

four

extended speaking

student B You're one of the students on the course and you're going to telephone the speaker and invite them to give their talk. Before you begin, plan what you're going to say and fill the gaps.

- Introduce yourself and explain why you're phoning.
- Give the speaker some details about the talk.

> The date of the weekend conference: _____
>
> Place: *the* _____ *Hotel*
>
> in _____ (name of town?)
>
> The audience will be _____
>
> _____ (who are they? how many?)
>
> The talk is 1 hour 15 minutes: you could use the 15 minutes for questions or discussion, starting at 2.00.
>
> You can offer the speaker a fee of _____ (how much?) for their talk.

- Be prepared to answer any other questions the speaker might have.
- Give them your e-mail address (write it here).

_____

eleven

reading
the camera never lies

text B

STRANGE AFFAIR OF THE KISS THAT WASN'T

There was always enormous competition between newspapers for photographs of Princess Diana with Dodi Fayed. In this one, *The Sun* newspaper decided to create its own picture. Under a headline 'Exclusive: The picture they all wanted', the paper showed Mr Fayed and the Princess about to kiss. However, the original picture (top) was weeks old and to make it look like a kiss, the newspaper was forced to **rotate** Mr Fayed's head. This picture later resulted in the creation of new rules concerning the **alteration** of photographs.

EXCLUSIVE: THE PICTURE THEY ALL WANTED

glossary
rotate turn round in a circular movement
alteration changing

eleven

how to ...
talk about a picture

eleven

extended speaking

student B Read this information and decide how to include it in the story of the man's life.

1 When he was at school, he and his friends hired a plane to take them to Paris for the day, which was against the school's rules.

2 After leaving school, he went to Oxford University but he was unable to finish his studies at that time because the war broke out.

glossary

broke out started

six

how to ...
enquire about a course

student A You're interested in doing a course in Art and Design, and you want to get a professional qualification. You've heard that there's a six-month course at your local college.

Before you begin, plan your questions. Here are three things you want to know:

– the fees for the course

– starting dates for the course

– the class size

Think of three more things you want to know.

_____

_____

_____

eight

how to ...
be a good guest

student A You're a student on a visit to Britain and you arrived at your landlord / landlady's home an hour ago. You have three things to talk about:

1 You've knocked over a vase of flowers in your bedroom, and there's a little water on the floor. Say sorry!

2 You brought a CD player with you and would like to play music in your room. Is that all right with the landlord / landlady?

3 You want to know if there's a bus or train into town.

You begin the conversation.

pairwork

six

how to ...
enquire about a course

student B You're the receptionist at a college and your college has two courses in Art and Design:

- a six-week course 'Basic Art and Design'
- a one-year course with a professional qualification 'Diploma in Art and Design'

Before you begin, fill the gaps below.

name of your college	
one-year course begins	
and ends	
full time course of	_hours per week_
cost of course is	
entry requirements	
number of students in class	
how to enrol	

Begin the phone conversation like this:

Hello, _____ College, how can I help you?

eight

how to ...
be a good guest

student B You're a landlord / landlady and your visiting student arrived an hour ago. They have some things they want to talk to you about. Before you begin, look at this information.

1 Noise is often a difficult subject with house guests. You want them to feel at home and to do what they like in their room. But they mustn't create a problem for the rest of your family, e.g. your husband / wife gets up very early to go to work.

2 Be ready to give your guest some directions and local transport information.

3 Your guest is going to eat with your family. Ask them if there's anything they don't eat or that they particularly like.

language reference

one

question forms

inversion

Auxiliary verbs and modal verbs usually come before the subject. For present simple and past simple, use *do / does / did*.

Are you leaving now?	**Has** he arrived?	**Do** you know her?
Did you like the film?	**Can** you speak Italian?	**Should** we tell her?

go to **exercise 1.1**

wh- / how questions

These words are used in questions which require specific information. Auxiliary verbs and modal verbs usually come before the subject.

What's he doing?	**When** can you do it?
Where does he live?	**Why** was he late?

Some *wh- / how* question words combine with other words.

How far can you see?	= distance
How long has he had it?	= length of time
How often do you go there?	= frequency
How much do you want?	= quantity (uncountable)
How many did you see?	= number (countable)
How old is he?	= age
What sort of car is it?	= specifying
What time did it start?	= point in time (when)

go to **exercise 1.2**

subject / object questions

When a *wh- word / how* ... is the subject of the sentence, it comes before the verb. Don't use *do / did*.

What happened?	– There was an accident. NOT ~~What did happen?~~
Who took my pen?	– Mary took it.
How many people came?	– About ten (did).

When a *wh- word / how* ... is the object, normal question word order is used with an auxiliary.

How many people did you see?	– (I saw) about ten.
When did you leave?	– (I left) around 6.30.
How often do you go?	– (I go) every week.

go to **exercise 1.3**

cover & check exercises

1.1 Correct the errors.
1 When he is leaving?
2 Where she lives?
3 Does he can speak German?
4 Did he came to see you?
5 They married?

1.2 What are possible questions for these answers?
1 It's twenty kilometres.
2 Three times a week.
3 I've got five.
4 Forty next week.
5 It's a Fiat.
6 About two hundred.
7 Midnight.
8 Since last year.
9 A litre.
10 Not long.

1.3 Make questions for these answers. Use the words in brackets.
1 I lost my bag. (What)
2 The brown leather one. (Which)
3 In the park. (Where)
4 Last Sunday. (When)
5 A small boy. (Who)

> Cover the grammar, then try the exercise. Check the grammar again to help you.

questions ending in prepositions

When the question word is the object of a preposition, the preposition usually goes at the end.

What are you looking **at**?

What did you do that **for**? = Why?

Who's she talking **to**?

go to **exercise 1.4**

question tags

These are used to check what you think is true, or to confirm information. You can use question tags to start a conversation or keep it going. To form question tags, repeat the auxiliary verb. If the auxiliary in the main clause is positive, the tag is negative; this is the most common pattern. If the auxiliary in the main clause is negative, then the tag is positive. If there's no auxiliary, use *do / does / did*.

It's really hot, **isn't it**?

We've met before, **haven't** we?

He **comes** from Israel, **doesn't** he?

You **aren't** married, **are** you?

You **can** swim, **can't** you?

She **passed**, **didn't** she?

If you think you know the answer and want confirmation, use falling intonation. If you're not sure about the answer, use rising intonation.

go to **exercise 1.5**

present perfect (1)

time up to now *have / has + past participle*

positive and negative forms			questions
I / you / we / they	**'ve** **haven't**	**met** him.	**Have** you **done** it?
he / she / it /	**'s** **hasn't**	**worked** well.	**Has** he **worked** there?

You can use the present perfect to talk about things that have happened in your life up to now. It isn't important when the things happened.

before now   now

I've written several books. = in my life; it isn't important when I wrote them

She's never **had** a holiday. = in her life, before now

The adverbs *ever*, *never*, and *before* are often used with the present perfect.

Have you **ever** been to Japan? = in your life

Have you been to Japan **before**? = before this occasion, before this trip

I've **never** read *War and Peace*. = not in my life

go to **exercises 1.6** *and* **1.7**

1.4 What are the missing prepositions in these questions?

1 What are they listening _____?
2 What did she buy that _____?
3 Who did you speak _____?
4 What is he talking _____?
5 What are they waiting _____?

1.5 Write the question tags.

1 They haven't finished, _____?
2 Peter can't drive, _____?
3 Marie's French, _____?
4 You work here, _____?
5 He's following me, _____?
6 You lost it, _____?
7 We're late, _____?
8 They shouldn't be here, _____?
9 He lives in London, _____?
10 She didn't marry him, _____?

When you've finished an exercise, say the sentences aloud.

1.6 Put *ever*, *never*, or *before* into these sentences.

1 Jenny's _____ been to India.
2 Have you eaten oysters _____?
3 I've _____ been late for anything.
4 Has John _____ read *War and Peace*?
5 I don't think we've met _____.

1.7 Make complete sentences. Use the present perfect and put *ever*, *never*, or *before* in the correct places.

1 You / see / this / man (before)?
2 Sue / drive / a car (never)
3 They / use / this / software (ever)?
4 Harry and Pam / meet (never)
5 He / tell / you / about it (ever)?

For a change, do an exercise quickly in your head.

Note: A common problem with the present perfect is with the construction *This / It is the first / second / only time I've been here*. A different tense is often used in other languages.

This is the first time I've done this. NOT ~~This is the first time I do this.~~
Is this the first time you've been abroad? NOT ~~Is this the first time you are abroad?~~
It's the only time I've been late. NOT ~~It's the only time I'm late.~~

go to **exercise 1.8**

recent events

You can use the present perfect to talk about things that happened a short time ago and are important now, often with *just*, *already*, and (*not*) *yet*.

It's **just** stopped raining.	⟶	so we can go out now
I've **already** had lunch.	⟶	I'm not hungry now
Haven't you finished that book **yet**?	⟶	I can see you're still reading it

go to **exercise 1.9**

present perfect v. past simple

When you give more specific information about where or when something happened, you usually use the past simple and not the present perfect.

A **Have you been** to Japan before?	B Yes, I **went** two years ago.
A **I've never met** Bill.	B Oh, really? I **met** him at Jill's party.

go to **exercise 1.10**

been and *gone*

Go has two past participles, *been* and *gone*. They have different meanings.

She**'s gone** to the theatre.	= She's at the theatre now.
He**'s been** to the shops.	= He went to the shops, and now he's back.

For more information on the **present perfect**, go to *p.157* and *p.166*.

go to **exercise 1.11**

future plans and intentions

going to + verb

positive and negative forms			questions
I	'm / 'm not	**going to** do it.	**Am I going to** do it?
You / we / they	're / aren't		**Are** you / we / they **going to** do it?
He / she / it	's / isn't		**Is** he / she / it **going to** do it?

You can use *be going to* + verb to talk about future plans and intentions. Don't use *will* + verb.

She**'s going to spend** a few days in Rome. = it's her plan
What **are** you **going to do** for your holidays this year? = what's your plan?
I've got plans for tonight – I**'m going to see** a film. = it's my intention
    NOT ~~I'll go to see a film.~~

go to **exercise 1.12**

1.8 Complete the sentences with the correct form of the verbs in brackets.

1 This is the first time I (try) yoga.
2 This is the third time we (travel) to India.
3 Is this the first time you (be) to the Taj Mahal?
4 It's the only time he ever (be) angry.
5 This isn't the first time I (see) this film.

1.9 Circle the correct adverb.

1 Haven't you finished already / yet?
2 I've yet / just had lunch.
3 Ben has already / yet seen that film.
4 It hasn't stopped snowing yet / just.
5 Oh, no! I've just / yet broken a glass.

1.10 Tick ✓ the correct sentences.

1 ☐ I've been to Holland last year.
   ☐ I went to Holland last year.
2 ☐ It's the first time I've been to Rome.
   ☐ It's the first time I'm in Rome.
3 ☐ I saw James at the wedding.
   ☐ I've seen James at the wedding.

1.11 What do these sentences mean?

1 *Julie has been to Egypt.*
   ☐ Julie went to Egypt and now she's back.
   ☐ Julie is in Egypt now.
2 *Mike's gone to the shops.*
   ☐ Mike is at the shops now.
   ☐ Mike went to the shops but now he's back.

1.12 Make questions using *going to* + verb.

1 It's Jon's party this evening. (What / wear?)
2 I've bought a new computer. (Where / put it?)
3 Mike's broken his leg. (How / get to work?)
4 We're both 30 on Saturday. (How / celebrate?)
5 Anna's won a lot of money. (What / do with it?)

plan, hope, and think

You can use other verbs to talk about your future plans and intentions, with different degrees of certainty.

I'm planning to take a few days off work soon.	=	it's my plan
We're hoping to open a new factory next year.	=	we want to, but we're not sure it will happen
I'm thinking of selling my computer.	=	I'm thinking about it as a future possibility

Hope and *plan* (but not *think*) can also be used in the simple form, with little change in meaning.

I **plan** to take a month off work in the summer.	I **hope** to see him soon.

For more information on **be going to**, go to *p.165*.

go to **exercise 1.13**

exclamations with *what* and *how*

what + a / an + countable noun	**what + a / an + adjective + noun**
What a surprise!	What a lovely dress!
What a shame!	What an interesting idea!
what (+adjective) + uncountable / plural noun	**how + adjective**
What rubbish!	How exciting!
What fantastic weather!	How incredible!
What noisy children!	

go to **exercise 1.14**

1.13 Rewrite the sentences. Use the verbs *think*, *plan*, or *hope*.

1 I want to go to France but I'm not sure it'll happen.
   I'm _____.
2 It's my plan to travel round Europe.
   I'm _____.
3 I may go to the cinema this evening.
   I'm _____.

> Is this grammar the same in your language? If not, make a note of the difference.

1.14 Tick ✓ the correct sentences and correct the others.

1 ☐ What fantastic day!
2 ☐ What pity!
3 ☐ How amazing!
4 ☐ What a terrible weather!
5 ☐ What a nightmare!
6 ☐ What great news!
7 ☐ What fascinating book!
8 ☐ How beautiful flowers!
9 ☐ What a shocking story!
10 ☐ What delicious cake!

---

two

comparative and superlative adjectives

form

One-syllable adjectives and two-syllable adjectives ending in -y:

adjective	comparative	superlative	notes
slow	slower (than)	the slowest	+er / +est
safe	safer	the safest	+r / +st
big	bigger	the biggest	double consonant after short vowels /ɪ/, /e/, /ɒ/, /æ/
noisy	noisier	the noisiest	change -y to -i, +er / +est
quiet	quieter	the quietest	a few two-syllable adjectives add +er / +est, e.g. clever, narrow

go to **exercise 2.1**

cover & check exercises

2.1 What are the comparative and superlative forms of these adjectives?

1 big
2 easy
3 strong
4 nice
5 cheap
6 happy
7 hot
8 late
9 lazy
10 narrow

Many two-syllable adjectives (e.g. ending *-ful, -less, -ing, -ed*) and longer adjectives:

adjective	comparative	superlative	notes
tiring	more tiring (than)	the most tiring	**more** (+); opposite **less** (−)
useful	more useful	the most useful	**the most** (+); opposite **the least** (−)
dangerous	more dangerous	the most dangerous	
reliable	more reliable	the most reliable	

irregular forms:

adjective	comparative	superlative
good	better (than)	the best
bad	worse	the worst
far	further	the furthest

After a comparative adjective, use *than*.

This room is **bigger than** I thought.
Trains are **more reliable than** buses.

After a superlative adjective, you normally use *in*, not *of*.

It's **the biggest** factory **in** the world.   NOT ~~of the world~~
She's **the youngest** student **in** the class.   NOT ~~of the class~~

You can also make comparative and superlative phrases with nouns.

We need **more time** to do it.   This paper has **the most information** in it.
I want **less work**, not more!   This job will bring you **the most money**.

go to **exercise 2.2**

modifying comparatives

Use *much*, *far*, and *a lot* to express a big difference between two things.
Use *a bit*, *a little*, and *slightly* to show a small difference.

A is **a lot / much / far** lighter than C.
B is **a bit / a little / slightly** heavier than A.
C is **a lot / much / far** heavier than B.

Note: *a bit* and *a lot* are more informal than the other forms.

go to **exercise 2.3** *and* **2.4**

present simple and continuous (1)

present simple

positive and negative forms		questions
I / you / we / they	**work** / don't work	Where **do** you **work**?
he / she / it	**works** / doesn't work	Where **does** your sister **work**?

The present simple tense describes things which are always true.

Yoko **comes** from Japan.   She **has** two brothers and a sister.

2.2 Fill the gaps with an appropriate word.

1 Shirley is much _____ than I am at maths.
2 Peter works harder _____ I do.
3 That's the _____ expensive thing I've ever seen!
4 She gave me _____ money than I needed.
5 Are we going to drive much _____ down this road?

Write in pencil, then you can rub out your answers and do the exercise again later.

2.3 Put the words in the correct order to form sentences.

1 Pat / slightly / taller / is / than / me
2 older / I / than / are / you / far / am
3 reliable / Liz / much / than / I / more / thought / is
4 further / the / is / house / a bit / away
5 a lot / expensive / should / be / it / than / that / is / more

2.4 Choose *much, far, a lot, a bit, a little* or *slightly* to complete the sentences. More than one answer is often possible.

1 Africa is _____ bigger than South America.
2 A grapefruit is _____ smaller than a melon.
3 Going by car is _____ slower than going by plane.
4 Iceland is _____ colder than Spain.
5 Silk is _____ more expensive than cotton.

It also describes things we think are permanent, or true for a long time.

| Maria **lives** in Barcelona. | Where **do** you **work**? |

It describes habits and things that happen regularly.

| We **go** to the South of France for our holidays most summers. |
| I usually **play** football at the weekends. |

For more information on the **present simple**, go to *p.164*.

go to **exercise 2.5**

present continuous (1)

positive and negative forms			questions
I	'm	working	Where **am** I **going**?
	'm not		
he / she / it	's	working	What's she **wearing**?
	isn't		
we / you / they	're	working	Where **are** you **working**?
	're not / aren't		

The present continuous describes things happening at this precise moment.

| Don't talk to me about it now; I**'m watching** the news. |
| Sorry, she can't come to the phone; she**'s having** a shower. |

go to **exercise 2.6**

It also describes temporary things happening around now, but not necessarily at this precise moment.

now

| I**'m studying** English this year. |
| They**'re repairing** the motorway near our house. |

For more information on the **present continuous**, go to *p.164* and *p.165*.

compound nouns

Two or three words often go together to make compound nouns. This is a common feature of English.

tea cup = a cup you drink tea from	**shoe shop** = a shop where you buy shoes
writing paper	**letterbox**
tourist information office	**mother-in-law**

Most compounds are written as two words.

| **traffic lights** | **bus stop** | **credit card** | **snack bar** |

Some short noun + noun compounds are written as one word.

| **bedroom** | **sunglasses** | **postman** | **toothpaste** |

A small number have hyphens.

| **make-up** | **T-shirt** | **X-ray** | **sister-in-law** |

If you aren't sure how to write a compound, use a dictionary to check.

go to **exercise 2.7**

2.5 Match the sentences below with the correct uses.

a always true
b permanent or true for a long time
c routines and habits

1 I often go to the cinema. ___
2 Fruit is good for you. ___
3 The leaves on this tree change colour in the autumn. ___
4 George lives on a Greek island. ___
5 They love each other. ___
6 I always eat fish on Fridays. ___
7 Tony has a dog. ___
8 We go walking in summer. ___
9 My brother never drives to work. ___
10 Do you usually work late? ___

2.6 Complete the sentences. Use a suitable verb in the present continuous.

1 I usually work three days a week but this week I _____ Monday to Friday.
2 Maria _____ an essay at the moment so she can't go out.
3 I'm _____ the bus to work this week. The car's being serviced.
4 It's very hot in my room so I _____ in the spare room at the moment.
5 Come in! Everyone _____ the match on TV.

For a change, do an exercise in your head.

2.7 Complete the compound nouns and decide if they are one word or two.

1 traffic _____
2 snack _____
3 coffee _____
4 writing _____
5 tooth _____
6 sun _____
7 bus _____
8 bath _____
9 post _____
10 shoe _____

three

present perfect and past simple (2)

The present perfect can describe something that started in the past and continues up to now.

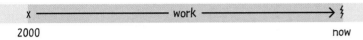

x ——————— work ————————→ ⚡	
2000	now

I've worked for this company since 2000. (I started in 2000 and I'm still here.)
I've worked there for a few years. (I started a few years ago and still work there.)

This use of the present perfect also describes something that <u>didn't</u> happen in a period of time from the past until now.

I haven't seen him since 1998. (The last time I saw him was in 1998.)
I haven't worked for five years. (I stopped working five years ago.)

If you want to describe something that started and finished in the past, use the past simple with *for* + a period of time. Compare:

She**'s had** that sports car for eighteen months. (present perfect: she still has the car.)
She **had** that motorbike for two years. (past simple: she hasn't got it now.)

x	motorbike	x	sports car	⚡
	two years		18 months	now

For and *since* are common with this use of the present perfect.

for + period of time	*since* + point of time
I haven't been **for three years / ages / a long time / a couple of weeks**.	I've known her **since last June / we were at school / last summer**.

go to **exercises 3.1** *and* **3.2**

The most common question with this use of the present perfect is *How long …?* This question can also be used with the past simple. Compare:

How long have you been a doctor? (I know you are a doctor now.)
How long were you in the army? (I know you aren't in the army now.)

For more information on the **present perfect**, go to *p.153* and *p.166*.

go to **exercise 3.3**

collocation

Collocation describes the way pairs or groups of words often go together.

verb + noun	noun + verb	adjective + noun	adverb + adjective
play the guitar	the car broke down	blonde hair	terribly sorry
take a photo	the bomb exploded	a close friend	completely empty

Many collocations are easy to understand. It can be difficult to produce them, however, because they don't always translate literally from different languages.

I missed the bus. NOT ~~I lost the bus.~~
She did her homework. NOT ~~She made her homework.~~
a fast train NOT ~~a rapid train~~
a terrible pain NOT ~~a strong pain~~

cover & check exercises

3.1 Correct the errors. Sometimes there's more than one possible answer.

1 I've lived here since three years.
2 She's bought that car three years ago.
3 I've been in Paris last weekend.
4 I didn't see Mark since Monday.
5 I wasn't there since last year.
6 Jane worked here since a month.
7 Mike's been on holiday last week.
8 I didn't see Jason since last year.
9 I enjoyed tennis when I've been a child.
10 We've seen our friends yesterday.

3.2 Put *for* or *since* in these sentences.

1 I haven't seen Isabelle _____ ages.
2 We've lived in this house _____ I was a baby.
3 Peter has known Sally _____ 1994.

3.3 Make questions for these answers. Use *How long …?* and the present perfect or past simple.

1 For fifteen years.
2 Since 1999.
3 For three months now.
4 For about a year or so.
5 Most of my adult life.

Is this grammar different in your language? If so, make a note of the difference.

A good dictionary will include common collocations often in **bold** type and in example sentences.

> friend /frend/ **noun** [C] a person that you know and like (not a member of your family), and who likes you: *Trevor and I are* **old friends**. *We were at school together.* • *We're only inviting* **close friends** *and relatives to the wedding.* • *Helen's my* **best friend**. • *A friend of mine told me about this restaurant.* • *One of my friends told me about this restaurant.* • ► Look at **boyfriend**, **girlfriend**, and **penfriend**. IDIOMS **be/make friends (with sb)** to be/become a friend (of sb): *Tony is rather shy and finds it hard to make friends.*

entry from Oxford Wordpower Dictionary ISBN 0194315169

go to **exercise 3.4**

used to + verb

positive and negative forms			questions
I / you / he / she / we / they	used to never used to* didn't use to	work	**Did** he **use to** work? **Did** they **use to** help?

* *Never used to* is more common in spoken English than *didn't use to*.

Use *used to* + verb to talk about past habits and states which are now finished or have changed. You can also use the past simple here.

She **used to** have a house in France, but she sold it a few years ago.
I **used to** wear suits a lot, but now I only wear them for special occasions.

Used to cannot describe how many times or how long something happened.

I **studied** German **for three years**. NOT I used to study German for three years.
I **went** to Greece **twice** for a holiday. NOT I used to go to Greece twice for a holiday.

Used to is not used to talk about the present. Use *usually* for this.

Nowadays people **usually** do a lot of their shopping in supermarkets.
    NOT Nowadays people usually used to do a lot of their shopping in supermarkets.

natural English ellipsis
You don't need to repeat the verb or phrase after *used to*.

A Do you ever go fishing?
B I **used to**, but I **don't** any more.

go to **exercises 3.5** *and* **3.6**

3.4 Complete these sentences with an appropriate word.
1 Jack's my closest _____ .
2 I'm terribly _____ I'm late.
3 When did you learn to _____ the drums?
4 Did you _____ many photos on holiday?
5 I'm late because I _____ the train.

3.5 Rewrite the sentences. Use *used to* + verb.
1 I played tennis a lot.
2 We went to Spain every year.
3 Patrick never liked Maths at school.
4 Anne had long hair.
5 You didn't go to the gym.

3.6 Tick ✓ the correct sentences and correct the others.
1 ☐ We used to go to Italy twice a year.
2 ☐ I used to go to Rome twice for a holiday.
3 ☐ I never used to take the bus. I always drove.
4 ☐ I don't use to play football these days.
5 ☐ Did you use to have short hair?

---

four

preferences

Use *would prefer to* + verb or *would rather* + verb to talk about a preference on a specific occasion.

A Would you like to go shopping today?
B I'**d prefer to go** to the beach. / I'**d rather go** to the beach.
A Do you want to order the books today?
B I'**d prefer to wait** until tomorrow. / I'**d rather wait** until tomorrow.

Would rather is more common than *would prefer to* in spoken English.

cover & check exercises

How do you talk about preferences in your language?

Prefer + *-ing* or *prefer* + full infinitive are used to talk about preferences in general. You don't usually use *would rather* for general preferences.

> On holiday, I **prefer to take** my car **than** to go by train.
> She **prefers** cross-country **skiing** to downhill **skiing**.

go to **exercise 4.1**

modal verbs *would, could / might*

positive and negative forms		questions
I / you / he / she / it / we / they	**would /'d** do it **wouldn't** do it **could** do it **couldn't** do it **might** do it **might** not do it	**Would** you do it? **Could** you do it?

natural English forms of *might*

It's more common and natural in English to say:

I **might not** come tomorrow.	than	I mightn't come tomorrow.
Do you think he **might** win?	than	Might he win?

Would and *could / might* often describe how certain you are in imaginary situations, for example:

> Chris likes his university course, but he hasn't got enough money.
> A friend suggests he gives up the course and works in a shop for a year.

Read what Chris says:

> **I'd (would)** have more money. = I'm sure about this
> I **wouldn't** enjoy working in a shop. = I'm sure about this
> It **could** be a way to save money and study next year. = this is possible
> I **might** be able to work part time and study. = this is possible

Compare these uses of *can* and *could* to express possibility.

> Madrid **can** be cold at this time of year. (It's sometimes cold; it's a fact.)
> Madrid **could** be cold at this time of year. (I imagine that it's possible.)

For more information on *could* and *might*, go to p.172.

go to **exercise 4.2**

modal verb *will* (1)

Use *will* (*'ll*) + verb when you're willing / happy and prepared to do things, e.g. promising, offering, or agreeing to do something. You often make the decision to do these things at the moment of speaking.

A	Is that the doorbell?	A	I need the books before tomorrow.
B	Yes, I**'ll** answer it.	B	OK, I**'ll** send them this afternoon.
	NOT ~~Yes, I answer it.~~		NOT ~~OK, I send them this afternoon.~~

Use *won't* when you're not willing to do things. Here it means 'refuse'.

> She **won't lend** me her laptop because I broke it last time.

For more information on *will*, go to p.165.

go to **exercise 4.3**

4.1 Make complete sentences using the infinitive or the *-ing* form of the verbs.

1 I'd rather (go) skiing than sailing.
2 I'd prefer (leave) early.
3 Would you rather (live) in France or Italy?
4 I much prefer (get up) early than late.
5 Jim always prefers (travel) by train.

4.2 Circle the correct modal verb.

1 It's difficult, but I would / might be able to do it.
2 Sarah could / would be upstairs. Have you looked?
3 I'm sure we might / would enjoy that.
4 I think this guide book might / can be useful for the trip.
5 I know I wouldn't / couldn't like it. I've tasted it before.
6 Pat would / might not come tomorrow. He's got a lot to do.
7 Would / Might you help me? This project is very difficult.
8 Do you think Alan can / might get the job?
9 He would / can hate working in an office. He likes being outside.
10 Jane looks pale. She could / would be ill or just tired.

When you've finished an exercise, say the sentences aloud.

4.3 Match the sentences below with the correct uses.

a offer or promise
b sudden decision
c unwillingness or refusal

1 I'm always nice to him, but he won't help me. ☐
2 Don't worry! I'll make sure your house is safe while you're away. ☐
3 That's the doorbell, isn't it? I'll see who's there. ☐

five

adjectives

You can use adjectives to modify nouns. They usually go before the noun.

a **wonderful** film   a **surprising** result   **horrible** weather   a very **old** friend

Some adjectives go after a noun, in the construction verb + object + adjective.

She left the window **open**.   That makes my father **angry**.

We use adjectives to modify certain verbs: *be, seem, look, sound, feel, become, get, go*. The adjectives go after the verb.

They **looked unhappy**.   That **sounds exciting**.
She's **getting tired** – let's go home.   He **was annoyed**.

go to **exercise 5.1**

adverbs of manner

	+*ly*				
adjective	perfect	easy	careful	gentle	
adverb	perfect**ly**	eas**ily**	careful**ly**	gent**ly**	
	irregular forms				
adjective	hard	fast	late	early	good
adverb	**hard**	**fast**	**late**	**early**	**well**

Not all words that end in -*ly* are adverbs; some are adjectives, e.g. *friendly, lovely, silly*.

You can use adverbs of manner to modify verbs. They usually come after the verb or the object.

Josh **played happily** with his toys.   You'd better **drive slowly**.
She shut **the door noisily**.   He left **the lesson early**.

Some adverbs can modify adjectives, past participles, and other adverbs.

It was **incredibly cold**.   These shoes are **well made**.
Sue did **very well** in the exam.   He's always **badly dressed**.

go to **exercises 5.2** *and* **5.3**

obligation and permission

must **and** *have to* **+ verb**

positive and negative forms		questions
I / you / we / they	**have to** do it.	**Do I have to** do it?
	must do it.	(**Must I** do it ...? is not common.
	don't have to do it.	Use **Do I have to ...?**)
	mustn't do it.	
he / she	**has to** do it.	**Does he / she have to** do it?
	must do it.	
	doesn't have to do it.	
	mustn't do it.	

cover & check exercises

5.1 Put the words in order.

1   very / sound / doesn't / he / pleased

   _____

2   mistake / made / a / she / bad / very

   _____

3   delicious / room / had / but / food / was /
    we / the / terrible

   _____

4   happy / made / the / prize / them / very

   _____

5   that / lovely / smells / soup

   _____

5.2 Make these adjectives into adverbs.

1   hopeful   _____
2   hard   _____
3   good   _____
4   simple   _____
5   easy   _____
6   late   _____
7   fast   _____
8   incredible   _____
9   nice   _____
10 horrible   _____

5.3 Fill the gaps with a suitable adverb.

1   Mary terrifies me. She drives too
    _____ .

2   It was good! My speech went rather
    _____ I thought.

3   She sings _____ and she's an
    awful dancer too.

4   Listen _____ . I'll explain it again.

5   I work far too _____ .

For a change, do an exercise orally with a partner. Check your answers, then write them in.

Remember that *have to* is a normal verb, and changes in the third person to *has to* / *doesn't have to*.

Use *must* and *have to* to express obligation: things that are necessary or important. *Must* is preferred for an obligation we feel ourselves. It is also used in written rules.

> I **must** try to eat more vegetables. (It's my opinion.)
> Applicants **must** fill in all the information correctly. (used on an official form)

Have to is used for external obligation.

> The doctor says I **have to** eat more fruit and vegetables.
>   (External obligation: the doctor says so.)
> You **have to** wear a seatbelt. (The law says so.)

Must and *have to* are often interchangeable, but *have to* is more common in conversation.

Mustn't and *don't have to* don't mean the same thing. *Mustn't* means that something is wrong, dangerous, or not permitted. *Don't have to* means that something isn't necessary.

> You **mustn't** leave young children on their own. (It's wrong and not permitted.)
> You **mustn't** take aspirin with alcohol. (It's dangerous.)
> You **don't have to** wear a tie if you don't want to. (It's not necessary.)
> You **don't have to** pay in some museums; they're free. (It's not necessary.)

natural English *have / haven't got to*

Have / haven't got to means the same as *have / don't have to*. It's usually only used in spoken English, where it's very common.

> I**'ve got to** finish my homework this evening.
> Fortunately we **haven't got to** sell the house now.

go to **exercises 5.4** *and* **5.5**

---

be allowed to + verb

positive and negative forms		questions
I	**'m / am not allowed to** do it.	**Am I allowed to** do it?
he / she	**'s / isn't allowed to** do it.	**Is he / she allowed to** do it?
you / we / they	**'re / aren't allowed to** do it.	**Are you / we / they allowed to** do it?

Remember that *be* is a normal verb, and changes in the third person to *is*.

Use *be allowed to* to talk about things you can do or are permitted to do.

> You**'re allowed to** take a dictionary into this exam.
>   (It's permitted. You can do it.)
> We **aren't allowed to** take these books out of the library.
>   (It's not permitted. We can't do it.)

Be careful!

> You**'re** not allowed to walk on the grass. NOT ~~It's not allowed to walk on the grass.~~

5.4 Circle the correct answers.

1 You mustn't / don't have to leave a dog in a hot car.
2 In Italy, you don't have to / mustn't spend a lot of money to eat well.
3 Peter mustn't / doesn't have to finish that report today. It can wait.
4 You don't have to / mustn't mix alcohol and medicines.
5 You mustn't / don't have to go if you don't want to.

5.5 Complete the sentences. Use *must, have to, mustn't,* or *don't have to*.

1 You _____ speak during a written exam.
2 In most countries, you _____ drive on the right.
3 All books _____ be returned before Friday.
4 I don't work on Sundays, so I _____ get up early.
5 If an accident is serious, you _____ tell the police.
6 You _____ to finish it today – you can do it tomorrow.
7 I really _____ stop smoking.
8 The doctor says I _____ look after my heart.
9 _____ you _____ wear smart clothes to work or can you wear jeans?
10 You _____ leave the car unlocked. Someone might steal it.

> If this grammar is different in your language, make a note of the difference.

should + verb

positive and negative forms		questions
I / you / he / she / it / we / they	**should** do it. **shouldn't** do it.	**Do you think I should** do it? (**Should I** do it? is less common.)

Use *should* to talk about things you believe are the correct or best thing to do. This may be a weak obligation or just advice. *Shouldn't* expresses something you think isn't correct or isn't a good idea.

> You **should** take an umbrella with you. (It's a good idea. It's going to rain.)
> You **should** dress smartly for an interview. (It's the correct thing to do.)
> You **shouldn't** put those books there. (It isn't the correct place for them.)
> You **shouldn't** park your car there; it isn't very safe. (It isn't a good idea.)

go to **exercise 5.6**

go to **exercise 5.6**

5.6 Rewrite the sentences. Use the correct form of *should(n't)* or *be allowed to*.

1 It isn't a good idea to park here.
You _____ .
2 You can't park here – there's a notice.
You _____ .
3 You can smoke in this room.
You _____ .
4 You mustn't wait here.
You _____ .
5 It's a good idea to eat less salt.
You _____ .

six

conditional clauses

zero conditional

if + present simple, present simple

If she **sleeps** badly, she**'s** tired the next day.
He always **gets** angry **if I arrive** late.

Use zero conditional sentences to talk about a situation that is always true. In this case, *if* means *every time this happens / every time this is true* or *when this happens*.

He always **gets** angry **if / when I arrive** late.
If / when you **leave** chocolate on the table, my brother **eats** it.

first conditional

if + present simple, *will / might / could* + verb

If I get lost, I**'ll ring** you on my mobile.
We **might go** to the coast **if** the weather is nice.

Use first conditional sentences to talk about the result of a possible future event or situation. If you're sure about the result, use *will / won't*. If you aren't sure, use *might / could*.

If you **finish** your homework quickly, you**'ll have** time to go to the cinema.
I **won't be** sorry **if** David **doesn't come**.

go to **exercises 6.1** *and* **6.2**

unless

I **won't go unless** they **invite** me.

Unless means *if not*.

He**'ll fail unless** he works harder. (He'll fail if he doesn't work harder.)

go to **exercise 6.3**

cover & check exercises

6.1 Write 0 (zero) or 1 (first) next to these conditional sentences.

1 If you go swimming, you get wet. ☐
2 If I don't feel tired later, I'll go out. ☐
3 If you leave that there, the dog will eat it. ☐
4 If you put sea water in the sun, you eventually get salt. ☐
5 We may go surfing if the waves are good. ☐

6.2 Match the sentence halves. More than one answer is sometimes possible.

1	I won't come	a	if you're late.
2	I'll ring you	b	if it's a nice day.
3	I'll lend you the money	c	unless you want me to.
4	I won't worry	d	if I get lost.
5	I'll get up early	e	if you promise to return it.

6.3 Circle the correct words in these sentences.

1 If / Unless you tell me, I'll never know!
2 I'll get up / I get up if you insist.
3 Kate will miss the bus unless / if she doesn't run.

if and *when*

In zero conditional sentences, *if* and *when* can usually both be used with the same meaning.

> He always **gets** angry **if / when** I **arrive** late.

In first conditional sentences *if* and *when* do not mean the same thing.

> I'll phone you **when** I get my results.   (**when** = I know that I'll get my results.)
> I'll phone you **if** I get my results tomorrow.
>   (**if** = I'm not certain that I'll get my results tomorrow.)

go to **exercise 6.4**

preposition + *-ing* forms

When a verb follows a preposition, use an *-ing* form, not an infinitive.

> Think carefully **before taking** such a big risk.
> **After leaving** the company, he went to the States.
> I can't type **without looking** at the keys.
> Patrick's particularly good **at interpreting** the law.
> We aren't in favour **of changing** the law.

go to **exercise 6.5**

6.4 Write *if*, *when*, or both.

1 I'll travel more _____ I get older.
2 _____ he does that again, I'll be furious.
3 Pat doesn't go out much _____ the weather is bad.
4 I'll be amazed _____ she passes her exams.
5 I'll get the money _____ the bank opens.

6.5 Complete these sentences with *after*, *before*, *without*, or *of* and the *-ing* form of the verb.

1 Think carefully _____ _____ (take) such a big risk.
2 The main advantage _____ _____ (work) from home is the peace and quiet.
3 _____ _____ (leave) the company, he went to the States.
4 Shall we get a take-away instead _____ _____ (cook)?
5 Can you stand on one leg for a minute _____ _____ (fall) over?

seven

verb patterns

When you learn a new verb, it's important to know the structure that follows it. Some verbs have more than one structure:

verb +	object	full infinitive	+ object + full infinitive
	He wants some help.	He wants to help her.	He wants me to help him.

It's best to use a dictionary to check.

verb +	*that*	*to do* sth	sb + *that*	*to* + sb/sth	sb (*not*) + *to do* sth
	say	decide	tell	write	tell
	explain	try	warn	speak	warn
	realize	refuse	advise	talk	advise
	suggest	offer	persuade	reply	persuade
		promise			ask
		want			**sb + *to do* sth**
		hope			want
		agree			invite
					allow

go to **exercises 7.1** *and* **7.2**

cover & check exercises

7.1 Correct the mistakes in these sentences. Sometimes there's more than one possible answer.

1 Adam said me he was leaving tonight.
2 I want that Peter goes now.
3 Ella told that she felt ill.
4 Guy advised to put the money in the bank.
5 My brother explained me that it was difficult.

7.2 Complete these sentences in your own words.

1 I realized …
2 Jack refused …
3 They warned …
4 You suggested …
5 She persuaded …
6 He allowed …
7 They advised …
8 He offered …
9 We told …
10 I explained …

present simple and continuous (2)

natural English present tenses in narrative

In spoken English, when you tell a story informally, tell a joke, or give a summary of a film, book etc., you can use the **present simple** and **present continuous**, instead of past tenses. This helps bring the story to life and makes it seem more immediate.

> At the beginning of the film, this couple **are sitting** in a field, and suddenly they **see** a hot air balloon come down near them, and a man **gets** out, and there's …

As you can see in the example above, the present continuous describes the scene. The present simple describes the series of actions (the narrative).

go to **exercise 7.3**

present continuous

When you're describing the action in a picture or things that are happening now, you can use the present continuous.

> In this photo, my brother**'s lighting** a barbecue and the children **are playing** football.

go to **exercise 7.4**

possessive 's

To talk about possession, you normally use *'s* (apostrophe *s*) after singular nouns and irregular plural nouns, and *s'* (s apostrophe) after regular plural nouns.

> **Peter's** brother   the **girls'** changing room (more than one girl)
> the **child's** bedroom   the **children's** bedroom (**children** is an irregular plural)

Compare:

> The **student's** marks (the marks of one student)
> The **students'** marks (the marks of several / all students)

When you're talking about things and not people, you usually use the preposition construction with *of*.

> the back page **of** the newspaper   NOT ~~the newspaper's back page~~
> the front door **of** the house   NOT ~~the house's front door~~

natural English 's for somebody's house or workplace

In conversation, you can use *'s* without a following noun to mean 'at somebody's home' or 'at somebody's shop / business'.

> I'm going to **Jane's** this evening.
> I've got to go to the **baker's / butcher's / dentist's / doctor's**.

go to **exercises 7.5** *and* **7.6**

7.3 Complete the story. Use the present simple and the present continuous.

At the start of the film, a man and a woman ¹ _____ (have) a meal in a restaurant, and they ² _____ (discuss) something. Suddenly, the waiter ³ _____ (interrupt) them and ⁴ _____ (tell) the man that there's a phone call for him. When he comes back to the table, the woman has gone, but her wedding ring ⁵ _____ (lie) on the table …

7.4 Write three things that are happening around you. Use the present continuous.

1 _____
2 _____
3 _____

7.5 Put an apostrophe in the correct places.

1 This is a postmans uniform.
2 Those are policemens uniforms.
3 Peter and John are Jennys sons.
4 The students test results were so bad he had to retake it.
5 This is the girls changing room.
6 Where are the childrens clothes?
7 I'm going to the doctors later.
8 Let's go over to Anns tonight.
9 Is this the womens fashion department?
10 Could you buy two steaks at the butchers, please?

7.6 Circle the correct words in each sentence.

1 What was the result of the match / the match's result?
2 Are we going over to Peter / Peter's tonight?
3 We climbed to the mountain's top / the top of the mountain.
4 Is that the car of Paul / Paul's car outside?
5 We've reached the end of the road / the road's end.

eight

present continuous and *be going to* + verb

When you're talking about plans or arrangements in the future, you can always use *be going to* + verb.

> She**'s going to visit** the castle tomorrow. (It's her plan.)
> They**'re going to meet** in a bar at 7.00. (It's an arrangement; they all know about it.)

natural English *going to* + verb

When the verb is *go*, it's much more natural to leave it out.

> I'm going to the cinema this evening.
>   NOT ~~I'm going to go to the cinema this evening.~~

When you're talking only about arrangements (and not plans), it's more common to use the present continuous than *be going to*.

> I**'m meeting** Bob tonight. (We arranged it together before.)
> We**'re having** lunch with my parents on Sunday. (They invited us before now.)
> I**'m seeing** my boss this afternoon. I**'m going to** ask him for more money. (it's my intention) NOT ~~I'm asking him for more money.~~

go to **exercises 8.1** *and* **8.2**

will and *be going to* + verb for prediction

positive and negative forms		questions
I / you / he / she / it / we / they	**'ll (will)** do it. **won't (will not)** do it.	**Will** you / he / they do it?

positive and negative forms			questions
I	**'m** / **'m not**	**going to** do it.	Are you **going to**?
he / she / it	**'s** / **isn't**		Is he / she / **going to**?
you / we / they	**'re** / **'re not**		

When you're making predictions using *will* / *be going to*, you can use both forms with the same meaning.

> I think she**'ll pass** the exam. I think she**'s going to pass** the exam.
> That **won't happen**, I'm sure. That**'s not going to happen**, I'm sure.
> I think the weather **will** probably **get better** later.
> I think the weather**'s** probably **going to get better** later.

With this meaning, *will* is more frequent than *be going to*, but both forms are common. *Probably* is often used in predictions. It goes after *will* or *be*.

When you're making a prediction based on present evidence, or you know that the prediction has already started to happen, use *be going to* rather than *will*.

> Look! He**'s going to score!**   My sister**'s going to have** a baby.

go to **exercises 8.3** *and* **8.4**

When *going to* is followed by a verb, it's often pronounced /ˈɡənə/.

> It isn't going to /ˈɡənə/ rain today.

cover & check exercises

8.1 Tick ✓ the sentences where you could use the present continuous.

1 ☐ I'm going to wash my hair this evening.
2 ☐ I'm going to have dinner with Tom tomorrow.
3 ☐ My boss has told me that I'm going to work in Bristol next week.
4 ☐ I've just had a great idea – I'm going to buy a boat.
5 ☐ I'm going to see the bank manager tomorrow.

8.2 Write two plans and one arrangement you have for the future.

1 _____
2 _____
3 _____

8.3 Substitute *be going to* with *will* where possible.

1 I think she's going to find the course very difficult.
2 Look at those clouds – it's going to rain.
3 That man is driving too fast: he's going to crash.
4 They say the economy isn't going to improve until next year.
5 I'm sure he's going to be here soon.

8.4 Use *will* or *be going to* to make complete sentences. Sometimes both are possible.

1 It / probably / rain / on my birthday. It usually does.
2 Look at that blue sky! It / be / a / nice / day.
3 Be careful! You / fall / off / that / ladder.
4 In 2035 / I / be / seventy.
5 I / be sure / she / win. / She's playing really well.

> Cover the grammar and try the exercise. Check the grammar again if you need to.

present perfect (3)

You can use the present perfect to talk about a past action when the results are important or evident now.

Look! **She's broken** the window. (There's broken glass on the floor.)
I've lost my keys. (I can't get into the house.)

Compare:

I **broke** the window, but my dad fixed it.
(The window isn't broken now, so it isn't important any more.)
I've broken the window and now I've got to pay for it. (The window is still broken.)

go to **exercise 8.5**

uncountable nouns

Uncountable nouns:

– aren't normally used with *a / an*.

furniture, research NOT ~~a furniture, a research~~

– are normally used with a singular verb.

the spaghetti is hot NOT ~~the spaghetti are hot~~

– don't usually have a plural form.

baggage, equipment NOT ~~baggages, equipments~~

A dictionary will tell you whether a noun is countable or uncountable.

★ information /ˌɪnfəˈmeɪʃn/ **noun** [U] information (on/about sb/sth) knowledge or facts: *For further information please send for our fact sheet • Can you give me some more information about evening classes in Italian, please?*
► The word **information** is uncountable so you CANNOT say: *I need an information*. You can, however, talk about **a bit** or **piece of information**.

★ chair¹ /tʃeə/ **noun 1** [C] a piece of furniture for one person to sit on, with a seat, a back and four legs: *a kitchen chair • an armchair*

entries from *Oxford Wordpower Dictionary* ISBN 0194315169

The uncountable nouns below are often countable in other languages.

weather	advice	accommodation	information
homework	luggage	baggage	progress
traffic	news	furniture	research
spaghetti	equipment	knowledge	money
machinery	toast	bread	work

go to **exercises 8.6** *and* **8.7**

8.5 Answer the questions Y (yes) or N (no).

1 'Excellent! David's just arrived.'
Is David here now? Y☐ N☐

2 'I've only been here five minutes and I've already broken three glasses.'
Are the glasses broken now? Y☐ N☐

3 'Typical! The tap's leaking and the plumber has gone home.'
Is the plumber still there? Y☐ N☐

8.6 Circle the correct words in the rules.

1 Uncountable nouns can be used with *a or an / the*

2 You use a singular / plural verb with uncountable nouns.

3 You can / can't put a plural *-s* on an uncountable noun.

8.7 Choose one of the words below and *some* or *the* to complete the sentences.

information	advice	furniture
news	research	

1 I wonder if you could give me
_____ _____ .

2 Have you heard _____ _____ ?
There's been a terrible flood.

3 I think Kathy is doing _____
_____ into genes.

4 Let's move _____ _____
outside while we paint the room.

5 Thanks. I think I have all _____
_____ I need now.

When you've finished an exercise, say the sentences aloud.

nine

second conditional

> For more information on **zero and first conditional**, go to *p.162*.

if + past simple, *would* / *might* / *could* + verb

> **If** I **knew** the answer, **I'd tell** you.
> You **might get** lost **if** you **went** that way.
> **If** you **got** the job, you **could move** out of town.

You can use this structure to describe present or future events that are unreal/imagined or improbable/unlikely to happen.

> **If** I **knew** the answer, **I'd tell** you.
> (I don't know the answer; I'm just imagining what I would do.)
> You **might get** lost if you **went** that way. (I know you probably won't go that way.)

Compare:

> **If** I **work** on Saturday, **I'll get** more money.
> (It's a real possibility that I'll work on Saturday.)
> **If** I **worked** on Saturday, **I'd get** more money.
> (It's very improbable that I'll work on Saturday.)

You can say *was* or *were* with *I*, *he*, *she*, and *it*.

> **If** I **was** / **were** more ambitious, I'd apply for that job.
> I'd be happier if he **was** / **were** here all the time.

go to **exercises 9.1** *and* **9.2**

To give advice, you can say *If I were you* ... . *If I was you* ... is possible, but some people do not consider it to be correct grammar.

> **If** I **were you**, I'd sell that car of yours.

go to **exercise 9.3**

prefixes

You can use these prefixes to give adjectives a negative meaning.

unhappy   **in**efficient   **im**possible   **il**logical   **ir**responsible   **dis**honest

- *un-* is the most common prefix and is used with a lot of adjectives:

  uncomfortable, unpopular, unfair

- *in-* is also quite common, particularly with words of Latin origin:

  inconvenient, indecisive, invisible

- *im-* is only used with adjectives beginning with *m* or *p*:

  immoral, impolite

- *il-* is only used with adjectives beginning with *l*:

  illegal, illegible

- *ir-* is only used with adjectives beginning with *r*:

  irrational, irresponsible

cover & check exercises

9.1 **Correct the errors.**

1   If you would know the answer, you could help me.
2   She might got angry if you told her that now.
3   If I'm you, I wouldn't accept that job.
4   If I had lots of money, I'll give up work.
5   If you were me, what do you do?

9.2 **Rewrite the sentences. Use the second conditional.**

1   I can't check the train times. I haven't got a timetable.
    If _____ .
2   He doesn't speak any English. It's difficult to communicate.
    If _____ .
3   He can't go out. He's got a bad cold.
    If _____ .
4   She won't go because the journey is too long.
    If _____ .
5   I'm not ambitious so I won't get promoted.
    If _____ .

9.3 **Read the problems. Give advice using** *If I were you* ...

1   I've forgotten my mother's birthday.
2   I've crashed my girlfriend's car.
3   I've broken a priceless vase in a shop.
4   I've lost the neighbour's rabbit.
5   I've upset my best friend.

For a change, do an exercise orally with a partner. Check your answers, then write them in.

– *dis-* is used with a limited range of adjectives:

> disobedient, disloyal

The prefix *dis-* is also used to give some verbs a negative meaning.

> **dis**like, **dis**agree, **dis**obey

Use *dis-* and *un-* to reverse the action of certain verbs.

> **dis**appear, **un**lock, **un**pack

go to **exercise 9.4**

adverbs of frequency

You can use these adverbs to talk about how often things happen:

always	almost always	normally usually	frequently often	quite often	sometimes	occasionally	rarely seldom hardly ever	never

go to **exercise 9.5**

Adverbs of frequency go:

– before the main verb.

> They **often** take the children to the beach.
> I **always** see them in town on Saturdays.

– after auxiliary or modal verbs (but before the main verb).

> I've **occasionally** seen rabbits in our garden.
> You can **hardly ever** find enough room to sit down in there.
> Do you **normally** eat so fast?

– after the verb *be*.

> She's **seldom** on time.

These adverbs can go at the beginning or end of a clause:

> usually, normally, frequently, often, quite often, sometimes, and occasionally.

> **Normally**, we have to put the rubbish out every evening.
> I like to eat out **sometimes**.

go to **exercises 9.6** *and* **9.7**

9.4 Write the opposite of these words. Use a prefix.

1 polite _____
2 convenient _____
3 pack _____
4 legal _____
5 appear _____
6 lock _____
7 efficient _____
8 agree _____
9 moral _____
10 rational _____

9.5 Fill the gaps in these sentences with a suitable adverb of frequency.

1 Luke is very annoying: he's _____ talking about himself.
2 I'm glad to say I've _____ been late for an appointment.
3 Lisa is very shy. She _____ goes out to parties.
4 We _____ go shopping on Saturdays. The town is too crowded.
5 Today I'm taking the bus to work but _____ I walk.

9.6 Put the words in the correct order to form sentences.

1 always / I / before / bed / go / midnight / to
2 take / dog / often / the / we / woods / to / the
3 so / fast? / you / normally / do / drive
4 I / written / have / articles / occasionally / it / about
5 seldom / his / entertaining / are / films

9.7 Put the adverbs in brackets in the correct place. More than one answer is possible for each one.

1 There is a good film on Sunday evening. (usually)
2 I wonder what life is all about. (sometimes)
3 I forget to lock my front door. (quite often)
4 We have friends round for a meal at the weekend. (normally)
5 You see foxes at the bottom of the garden. (occasionally)

articles

the definite article *the* or zero article

When you talk about people or things in general, you don't usually use *the* with uncountable or plural nouns.

I don't think money (NOT ~~the money~~) is the most important thing in life (NOT ~~the life~~).
Girls (NOT ~~The girls~~) grow up more quickly than boys (NOT ~~the boys~~).

When you talk about someone or something specific, you usually use *the*.

The money she lent me is in my briefcase. (We know which money the person means.)
The girls in my class are French. (We know which girls she is talking about.)

go to **exercise 10.1**

the v. the indefinite article *a / an*

If people or things aren't defined or we haven't heard about them before, we use *a / an*.

A man and **a** woman were sitting in a park. (We haven't heard about them before.)
I bought **a** lovely coat yesterday. (This is the first time I've spoken about the coat.)

Use *the* when you know which one(s) you're talking about because:

– you've heard about it / them before.

  A man and **a** woman were sitting in a park. **The** man suddenly got up and …

– it's defined in the context.

  What happened to **the** book I lent you?

– it's the only one in the context.

  Where's my book?
  Oh, you left it in **the** kitchen. (There's only one kitchen in this context.)

go to **exercise 10.2**

determiners *all*, *most*, and *some*

You can use *all*, *most*, and *some* before a plural countable noun or an uncountable noun to talk about things in general.

| All / Most / Some | students work hard. |
| | work is boring. |

You can use *all*, *most*, and *some* to talk more specifically.

All (of) the students in the room have finished the exam.*
Most of the people I know work hard.
Some of the passengers were hurt in the accident.

* You can leave out *of* after *all* when it's followed by a noun, but not a pronoun:

  All (of) the children arrived late.   **All of them** arrived late.

You don't say ~~all people~~. You should usually say *everyone / everybody*.

go to **exercise 10.3**

cover & check exercises

10.1 Cross out any definite articles that are not necessary.

1 The love is the most important thing in life.
2 I think the money is the problem with society.
3 Generally girls are more mature than the boys.
4 The oranges are good for you: they're full of vitamins.
5 I'm very happy with the life at the moment.

10.2 Complete the gaps with *a*, *an*, or *the*.

I went to see ¹___ film yesterday with ²___ old friend. It was about ³___ man and ⁴___ young girl who survived ⁵___ plane crash. ⁶___ man carried ⁷___ girl for over twenty kilometres, until they got to ⁸___ small village. Unfortunately, no one would help them because they didn't believe ⁹___ story about ¹⁰___ plane crash so they had to …

Write in pencil, then you can rub out your answers and do the exercise again later.

10.3 Rewrite the sentences. Use *all*, *most*, or *some*.

1 I had five apples. I ate five apples.
  I ate _____ .
2 We invited twenty children to the party. Eighteen came.
  _____ to the party.
3 I made forty sandwiches. They ate ten.
  _____ the sandwiches.
4 There are ten people in the judo class. Ten turned up today.
  They _____ .
5 Ten people came to dinner. Five arrived late.
  _____ arrived late.

defining relative clauses

A relative clause gives more information about something in the main clause. Defining relative clauses tell us which specific (kind of) person or thing you're referring to. Use *who/that* to refer to people, and *which/that* to refer to things.

She's the woman **who/that** gave me the money.

main clause   defining relative clause

David's the boy **who/that** I told you about.
What time's the programme **which/that** you want to see?
I only watch films **which/that** make me laugh.

Who, *which*, and *that* can be the subject or object of the clause.

I always thank people for the help *(that)* they've given me. (*that* is optional.)
                                    object subject verb

I always thank people *that/who* help* me. (*that/who* is necessary.)
                      subject verb object

* Notice you cannot omit *who/which/that* when they're followed by a verb.

Don't use another pronoun (e.g. *it, him*) with the relative pronoun.

She's the woman who lives in that house.
   NOT She's the woman who she lives in that house.
He's the doctor who my father talked about.
   NOT He's the doctor who my father talked about him.

natural English *who v. whom*

If *who* or *that* are the object of the clause, *whom* is also possible but very formal.

I'd like you to meet Mr Custer,
   whom I first met at the Paris conference. = formal
   who I first met at the Paris conference. = conversational

go to **exercises 10.4** *and* **10.5**

10.4 Fill the gaps with a relative pronoun.

1 That's the dog _____ bit me.
2 Melissa is the girl _____ I was talking about yesterday.
3 I never read books _____ have sad endings.
4 Mrs Chumley is the woman _____ lent me this machine.
5 The hard drive is the bit _____ stores the information.

10.5 Join these sentences together. Use a relative clause.

1 I bought a ring. It cost over £200.
   _____

2 I took the medicine. The doctor recommended it.
   _____

3 I rang the man. I had met him at the party.
   _____

4 I work for a company. It makes microchips.
   _____

5 I spoke to the people. They live next door.
   _____

suffixes

Suffixes are used to change words from one grammatical category to another.

forming nouns

adjectives	dark	tolerant	confident	punctual	honest
nouns suffix	-ness	-ance	-ence	-ity	-y
nouns	darkness	tolerance	confidence	punctuality	honesty

verbs	improve	invite	elect	teach/act
nouns suffix	-ment	-ation	-ion	-er/or
nouns	improvement	invitation	election	teacher/actor

forming adjectives

nouns/verbs	comfort	fame	democrat	logic	create
adjective suffix	-able	-ous	-ic	-al	-ive
adjectives	comfortable	famous	democratic	logical	creative

Make a note of other words you know that change when you add a suffix.

forming verbs

nouns / adjectives	modern	strength
verb suffix	-ize	-en
verbs	modernize	strengthen

Some suffixes have a specific meaning.

-less can mean 'without'.

careless	painless	useless	homeless

Often (but not always) -ful means the opposite of -less.

careful = full of care	painful	useful	~~homeful~~

-able / -ible sometimes means 'can be done'.

unbreakable = cannot be broken	washable	drinkable	comprehensible

go to **exercises 10.6** and **10.7**

10.6 Form nouns from these words.

1 modest ___
2 weak ___
3 educate ___
4 confident ___
5 punctual ___
6 important ___
7 popular ___
8 arrange ___
9 sad ___
10 patient ___

10.7 Put a suitable adjective in these sentences. Use these words to help you.

democrat   thought   create   danger   music

1 Bungee-jumping looks extremely _____ to me.
2 Sophie is a very _____ child. She sings and she plays the flute.
3 I wish I were more _____ . I can't paint or draw.
4 I'm so glad I live in a _____ country.
5 Jeff is very _____ . He's always kind and considerate.

eleven

passive forms

	be + past participle	
present simple	it's (is) made	
present continuous	it's being sold	
past simple	he was arrested	they were told
present perfect	I've been invited	it's (has) been sold
future simple	he'll be understood	

When you use the passive form, you're often more interested in what happens to somebody or something than who did the action.

passive   The child **was sent** to a private school outside the town.
(We're more interested in what happened to the child.)

active   The Browns **sent** all their children to state schools.
(We're more interested in what the Browns did.)

If you want to say who performed an action, it's more common to use the active form. However, it's also possible to say who did the action using by + noun.

The police told the family about the robbery.
The family **was told** about the robbery **by the police**.

Only use by + noun when it's important or unusual information. Don't use it if it's clear from the context.

The robber was arrested ~~by the police~~.
The injured man was taken to hospital ~~by the ambulance~~.

go to **exercises 11.1** and **11.2**

cover & check exercises

11.1 Circle who or what is doing the action.

1 He took his son to the station.
2 Tom was bitten by a dog.
3 I was woken by the baby crying.
4 The train pulled out of the station.
5 By six o'clock, we were travelling down the motorway.
6 Someone broke into the museum.
7 The rings were stolen by the burglars.
8 The volcano erupted last night.
9 The village was covered by the lava.
10 This book is published by Oxford University Press.

11.2 Complete the sentences. Use the correct form of the verb in brackets.

1 At the moment all the phone lines _____ (use).
2 This floor _____ (just / clean) but it still looks dirty.
3 The announcement _____ (make) tomorrow.
4 Most of our products _____ (export).
5 The house _____ (sell) last week.

The passive form is more common in formal situations, e.g. notices, newspaper reports.

> Visitors **are requested** not to take photographs inside the museum.
> After the new hospital **was** officially **opened**, the Prime Minister **was given** a tour of the building.

go to **exercise 11.3**

look, *look like*, and *look as if*

Use *look* + adjective to describe how things seem.

> She **looked angry** when I gave her the news.

Don't confuse this with *look* = use your eyes, which can be followed by an adverb.

> She looked at me angrily.

Use *look like* + noun to say two things appear similar.

> That man **looks like** my brother.
> The picture **looks like** a photograph, but it isn't.

Use *look as if / look as though* + clause to suggest something is true or possible.

> You **look as if** you're going to cry.   It **looks as though** it's going to rain.

go to **exercise 11.4**

modal verbs of deduction *must*, *could*, *may*, *might*, and *can't*

You can use these verbs to say how probable or certain something is, based on what you know or believe.

is	must (be)	could (be)	can't (be)	isn't
		may (be)		
		might (be)		

He's 60. (He told me he was 60 and I believe him.)
He **must** be at least 60. (He says he's a bit older than my mum, who's in her late 50s.)
He **could / may / might** be about 60. (I've seen photos of him; he looks about 60.)
He **can't** be 60. (His mother is 70.)
He **isn't** 60. (He told me he was 58 and I believe him.)

go to **exercise 11.5**

natural English ellipsis

You can avoid repetition like this:

A Is Rob in the office today?
B Yes, he **must be** ~~in the office today~~. His computer's on.

11.3 Make these active sentences passive.

1 They arrested the robber.
2 Someone cleaned up the town centre.
3 They print the books in Hong Kong.
4 Someone took a photo of the murder scene.
5 Someone showed the Prime Minister round the hospital.

11.4 Correct the errors in these sentences.

1 They don't look very happily, do they?
2 She looks like beautiful.
3 It looks as they are going to a party.
4 They looks like a group of tourists.
5 He looks as a rich man.

> Translate these structures into your language. Are they similar?

11.5 Fill the gaps. Use *must*, *might*, or *can't*.

1 She's wearing a wedding ring so she _____ be married.
2 Tim _____ be at the office but I'm not sure.
3 This insect has only got six legs so it _____ be a spider.
4 The shop is closed so he _____ be there.
5 I _____ have some small change but I'm not certain.

twelve

past perfect simple

positive and negative forms			questions
I / you / he / she / we / they	had / 'd hadn't	(+past participle) done it.	Had you / he / she done it?

Use the past perfect simple to describe a past event or situation and to show that another past event / situation happened earlier.

I left my briefcase on the train.   I suddenly remembered it.   now

I suddenly remembered I'd left my briefcase on the train.

Compare:

The doctor **had** already **left** when Jo arrived. (First the doctor left; then Jo arrived.)
The doctor **left** when Jo arrived. (Jo arrived; after that, the doctor left.)

Already is used with perfect tenses to emphasize that something happened earlier. It usually goes between *had* and the past participle.

I'd already gone to bed when Dan came home.

In sentences with the conjunctions *before* and *after*, the order of events is often clear, so the past perfect is optional.

The accident **(had) happened** before we arrived.

The past perfect is often used after verbs related to thinking e.g. *remember, realize, discover, wonder, find out, learn, think*.

I **realized** we'd **met** somewhere before.
I **found out** later that he'd **lied** to me.

go to **exercises 12.1** *and* **12.2**

phrasal verbs

There are different forms of phrasal verb.

verb +	particle	preposition	adverb + preposition
	Take off your jacket. The car **broke down**.	He **looked after** the child.	We've **run out of** oil. I **get on** well **with** Chris.

The meaning of some phrasal verbs is similar to the base verb.

He **stood up** when I came in.   Could you **tidy up** your room?

go to **exercise 12.3**

But often the meaning of a phrasal verb is different from the base verb.

They **carried on** talking. (They continued.)   He **gave up** smoking. (He stopped.)

natural English phrasal verbs in conversation

Most phrasal verbs are more common in informal speech than formal speech or writing. One-word verbs with a similar meaning are often more formal.

Fill in the form, then give it to me.   They **turned down** my offer.
Please **complete** the form in ink.   They **rejected** my offer.

cover & check exercises

12.1 Which explanation is correct?
Tick ✓ the box.

1 When I got to the bank it had already closed.
    A ☐ The bank closed before I arrived.
    B ☐ I arrived and then the bank closed.

2 I arrived at the party but John had left.
    A ☐ I arrived and then John left.
    B ☐ First John left, then I arrived.

3 The lesson had already started when there was a power cut.
    A ☐ First there was a power cut, then the lesson started.
    B ☐ The lesson started, then there was a power cut.

12.2 Correct the errors where necessary. Some sentences are correct.

1 I couldn't go to the restaurant because I spent all my money.
2 When I had arrived, the others had already left.
3 I gave him the money before he asked me for it.
4 When the film started, I realized I saw it a year ago.
5 I thought he'd been to Italy before, but I was wrong.

12.3 Complete these sentences. Use each verb once.

hurry   save   stand   tidy   sit

1 Please _____ up when the Prime Minister arrives.
2 Do _____ down and be quiet.
3 Would you _____ up the kitchen, please?
4 _____ up, otherwise we'll be late.
5 What are you _____ up for?

Some verbs are **intransitive** and don't take an object.

The car **broke down**.	I **woke up** at 7.00.

Other verb are **transitive** and take an object.

She **put on** her shoes.	He **gave** the money **back**.

With some transitive verbs, you can separate the verb and adverb using a noun or noun phrase.

Take off your jacket.	He **sent back** the broken TV.
Take your jacket **off**.	He **sent** the broken TV **back**.

If the object is a pronoun, it must go between the verb and adverb.

Pick the coat **up**.	**Pick it up**. NOT ~~Pick up it~~.
Take the books **back**.	**Take them back**. NOT ~~Take back them~~.

Use the examples in your dictionary to check how to use a phrasal verb in a sentence.

PHRASAL VERBS **call by** (*informal*) to make a short visit to a place or person as you pass by: *I'll call by to pick up the book on my way to work.*
call for sb (*Brit*) to collect sb in order to go somewhere together: *I'll call for you when it's time to go.*
call for sth to demand or need sth: *The crisis calls for immediate action.* • *This calls for celebration!*
call sth off to cancel sth: *The football match was called off because of the bad weather.*
call sb out to ask sb to come, especially to an emergency: *We had to call the doctor out in the middle of the night.*

entry from *Oxford Wordpower Dictionary* ISBN 0194315169

go to **exercises 12.4** *and* **12.5**

plural nouns

Some nouns are always plural, and always need a plural verb.

things we wear

jeans	(sun)glasses	trousers	tights	knickers
shorts	swimming trunks	(under)pants	pyjamas	

other common items

stairs	thanks	scissors	people	surroundings	goods	clothes

Your **sunglasses are** on the bed.	The **goods were** sent yesterday.

With the things we wear above, you can use *some* or *a pair of* before the noun to refer to a single item. You can use a number with *pairs of* to show how many.

I need **a** new **pair of** trousers.	I'll have to get **some** shorts.
She bought **three pairs of** tights.	

Some nouns end in -s, but are singular and need a singular verb.

news	athletics	gymnastics	physics	maths/mathematics	politics

I don't like **physics**.	NOT ~~I don't like physic.~~
Mathematics is very difficult.	NOT ~~Mathematics are very difficult.~~

go to **exercise 12.6**

12.4 Replace the underlined verbs with phrasal verbs. Make any necessary changes to the word order.

1 Please <u>remove</u> your helmet before coming into the bank.

_____

2 I <u>returned</u> to the post office with the parcel.

_____

3 We have to <u>complete</u> this questionnaire.

_____

4 It was midnight but I <u>continued</u> working.

_____

5 I'll <u>collect</u> you from the station.

_____

12.5 Can the underlined words change position in the sentence? Tick ✓ the box if they can.

1 ☐ She sent <u>back</u> the CDs that she didn't want.
2 ☐ The children ran <u>across</u> the road.
3 ☐ Did he pay <u>back</u> the money?
4 ☐ He turned <u>down</u> the music.
5 ☐ The plane took <u>off</u> very late.

A good dictionary will tell you the meaning of most phrasal verbs.

12.6 Circle the correct answer.

1 Could you pass me the scissor / scissors?
2 Those people is / are looking at us.
3 My jeans is / are in the wash.
4 Politics isn't / aren't very interesting.
5 Her trousers was / were very expensive.
6 The surroundings is / are magnificent.
7 I need a new shorts / pair of shorts
8 Mathematics have / has always driven me mad.
9 Thanks is / are due to Mr Jakes for organizing the event.
10 You must get some / a new clothes.

What other phrasal verbs do you know? Make a note of them.

irregular verbs

verb	past simple	past participle
be	was / were	been /bɪn/
beat	beat	beaten
become	became	become
begin	began	begun
bite /baɪt/	bit /bɪt/	bitten
blow	blew /bluː/	blown
break	broke	broken
bring	brought /brɔːt/	brought
build /bɪld/	built	built
burn /bɜːn/	burnt / burned	burnt / burned
buy	bought /bɔːt/	bought
can	could /kʊd/	could
catch	caught /kɔːt/	caught
choose /tʃuːz/	chose /tʃəʊz/	chosen
come	came	come
cost	cost	cost
cut	cut	cut
do	did	done
draw	drew /druː/	drawn
dream	dreamt /dremt/ / dreamed	dreamt / dreamed
drink	drank	drunk /drʌnk/
drive	drove	driven
eat	ate /et/ or /eɪt/	eaten
fall	fell	fallen
feed	fed	fed
feel	felt	felt
fight /faɪt/	fought /fɔːt/	fought
find	found	found
fly	flew /fluː/	flown
forget	forgot	forgotten
forgive	forgave	forgiven
freeze	froze	frozen
get	got	got
give	gave	given
go	went	been /bɪn/ / gone
grow	grew /gruː/	grown
have	had	had
hang	hung /hʌŋ/	hung
hear	heard /hɜːd/	heard
hide /haɪd/	hid /hɪd/	hidden
hit	hit	hit
hold	held	held
hurt /hɜːt/	hurt	hurt
keep	kept	kept
know	knew	known
lead /liːd/	led /led/	led
learn	learnt / learned	learnt / learned
leave	left	left

verb	past simple	past participle
lend	lent	lent
let	let	let
light	lit	lit
lose /luːz/	lost	lost
make	made	made
mean /miːn/	meant /ment/	meant
meet	met	met
pay	paid	paid
put	put	put
read /riːd/	read /red/	read
ride /raɪd/	rode	ridden /ˈrɪdən/
ring	rang	rung /rʌŋ/
rise	rose	risen /ˈrɪzən/
run	ran	run
say	said /sed/	said
see	saw	seen
sell	sold	sold
send	sent	sent
set	set	set
shoot	shot	shot
show	showed	shown
shut	shut	shut
sing	sang	sung
sit	sat	sat
sleep	slept	slept
smell	smelled / smelt	smelled / smelt
speak	spoke	spoken
spend	spent	spent
spill	spilled / spilt	spilled / spilt
split	split	split
stand	stood	stood
steal	stole	stolen
stick	stuck /stʌk/	stuck
swim	swam	swum /swʌm/
take	took	taken
tear /teə/	tore /tɔː/	torn /tɔːn/
tell	told	told
think	thought /θɔːt/	thought
throw	threw /θruː/	thrown
understand	understood	understood
wake	woke	woken
wear /weə/	wore /wɔː/	worn /wɔːn/
win	won /wʌn/	won
write	wrote	written

OXFORD
UNIVERSITY PRESS

Great Clarendon Street, Oxford OX2 6DP

Oxford University Press is a department of the University of Oxford.

It furthers the University's objective of excellence in research, scholarship, and education by publishing worldwide in

Oxford New York

Auckland Bangkok Buenos Aires Cape Town Chennai Dar es Salaam Delhi Hong Kong Istanbul Karachi Kolkata Kuala Lumpur Madrid Melbourne Mexico City Mumbai Nairobi São Paulo Shanghai Singapore Taipei Tokyo Toronto

with an associated company in Berlin

Acknowledgements

The Publisher and Authors are grateful to the following for permission to reprint copyright material:

pp.26/27 News International Syndication for extracts from article by Adam Fresco: 'From our man in paradise', *The Times*, London, 12.12.98, copyright © Times Newspapers Ltd, 1998; p.47 The Independent/Syndication for adapted article by Jonathan Glancey: 'Aargh! All I want is a cup of tea!', *The Independent*, 20.02.93; pp.104/105 Atlantic Syndication Partners/Evening Standard for extracts from article by Ed Harris: 'What do you do when you're stuck in a jam?', *Evening Standard*, 25.09.98; p.139 The Guardian for extracts from article: 'How much pocket money should you give?', *The Guardian* 21.06.00, copyright © The Guardian 2000; listening booklet p.10 International Music Publications Ltd for lyrics of 'A Perfect Day' by Lou Reed, copyright © 1973 Screen Gems-EMI Music Inc and Oakfield Avenue Music Ltd, USA, Screen Gems-EMI Music Ltd, London, WC2H OQY. All rights reserved; Phonemic chart reproduced with the kind permission of Adrian Underhill and available from Macmillan ELT.

Recordings directed by Martin Williamson, Prolingua Productions. Technical presentation by Leon Chambers, recorded at The Soundhouse Ltd.

Illustrations by Claire Bretécher
pp.2 (Agrippine reading), 3 (Byron with present), 4 (Agrippine with friend on bench and Agrippine with friend), 5 (Agrippine with friend), 6/7, 8/9, 32/33, 56/57, 80/81, 102/103, 124/125 and cover illustrations copyright © Claire Bretécher 2002.
Combined work (text and illustrations) copyright © Oxford University Press 2002.

Other illustrations
Wendy Blundell pp. 60/61, 140; Stefan Chabluk p.30; Cyrus Deboo pp.28, 49; Bob Dewar pp.4, 92, 93; Mark Draisey pp.3, 44, 45; Tony Forbes pp.118/119; Neil Gower pp.18, 94; Kveta pp. 46, 64, 110; Belle Mellor pp.47, 58, 59, 83; Jacqui Paull pp. 11, 12, 51; Roger Penwill pp.3, 68, 69; Gavin Reece pp.25, 40, 96, 99, 105, 116, 138; Chris Robson pp.106, 112; Martin Shovel pp.2, 20, 21; Harry Venning pp.5, 114, 115; Kath Walker pp.5, 134, 135; Jonathan Williams p.62; Lee Woodgate pp.36/37, 90.

Commissioned photography by:
Gareth Boden; Art direction by: Geri May
With additional thanks to: The Curve Bar Brighton; The English Language Centre, Hove; E-Horizon Internet Café Brighton; The Tin Drum Brighton

Picture research by:
Geri May

The Publisher and Authors would like to thank the following for permission to reproduce photographs:

BBC p.12 (Peter Sissons), p.49 (Jeremy Clarkson, animal psychologist, Ray Mears), p.55 Jamie Oliver, pp.132/133 (Ludovic Kennedy – Time Out, Your Witness); Private Collection/Bridgeman Art Library/DACS p. 39 (Rothko painting), Prado, Madrid/Bridgeman (Goya –Blind Man's Buff), Private Collection/Bridgeman Art Library/DACS (Picasso – bust of woman in blue hat); Britstock p.10 (Roger Cracknell/friends chatting), 22 (Mountain stock/Steam train, Fritz Schmidt/Microlight); Bubbles Photo Library p.70 (J.Woodcock/6th form classroom and school gates, Pauline Cutler/exam results); Cheltenham Art Gallery and Museum/The Bridgeman Picture Library/DACS p.131 (Village gossips/Stanley Spencer); Corbis: pp.13 (Laurence Manning/people on bus), 30 (holiday complex), 54 (Southern Stock/newspapers), 66/67 (Bob Krist/bar on Duval Street and Sloppy Joe's restaurant California); Evening Standard newspaper/Oliver Lim p.13; Getty images: cover (Whit Preston/blue sky), cover and throughout (Uwe Krejci/2 people), 6 and throughout (Rutz Manfred/ear), 10 (David Lees/Friends talking, woman laughing), 12 (Paul Viant/shopping, football), 13 and throughout (Alexander Walter/reading newspaper), 16 and throughout (Photodisc/finger on map), 17 (Donata Pizzi/girl, Antonio Mo/young man), 18 and throughout (Stephen Simpson/speaking woman), 23 Oliver Pinchart/tandem, 34 (Chad Ehlers/hammock, Romilly Lockyer/couple in autumn, Dan Charkin/people in art gallery, interior of nightclub), 35 (Ken Charnus/man), 40 Hulton, Dave Harris/Paul McCartney, 42 (Colour Day/Woman), 48 (Juan Silva/cat scene), 52 (VCC Tipp Howell/Businessman), 53 (Romilly Lockyer/Businessman conference), 70 (Stewart Cohen/science lab, David Paul/student in library), 71 (Tony Anderson), 72 (Bob Torrez/boy, Leland Bobbe/girl), 74 (Britt Erlanson), 75 (Daniel Bosler), 76 (Antonio Mo), 79 (Tomoko Hirano), 85 (David de Lossy/cinema, Michael Goldman/park, Brown W Cannon III/coffee bar, Romilly Lockyer/watching TV) 94 (Julie Toy/man), 95 (Frans Lemmens/Sugar Loaf mountain), 99 (G & M David de Lossy/iron, Bernhard Lang/computer, Ian Logan/espresso machine), 100 (Philip Lee Harvey/3 men, Marcus Lyon/businesswoman), 104 (John Laurance/traffic jam), 105 (glamorous woman, bus driver, Barry Rosenthal/Asian businessman), 106 (Simon Bottomley), 111 (Charbruchen/English teacher), 117 (Stuart McClymon/party), 118 (Yellow Dog/primary school teacher, Karen Beard/soldiers), 120/121 (Gábor Ekecs/expensive restaurant, Uwe Krejci/friends in restaurant, David de Lhossy/pop concert), 122 (Carol Kohen/couple cooking), 123 (Simon Battensby/using laptop, Colin Hawkins/couple laughing), 126 (Carol Kohen), 138 (Wendy Ashton/man 40's), Colour Day/woman 35, Michael Krasonitz/woman 55), 140 (Alan Danahar); The Guardian p. 46 (David Sillitoe/Jonathan Glancey); Hobsons p.107 (Ralph van Dijk); Impact pp.66 (Mike McQueen/cosy pub), 142 (Bruce Stephens); The Independent Newspaper pp.126, 127, 146, 148 (manipulated image); JCM Personal management p.107 (Jeff Harding); Kobal p.88 (Columbia/When Harry met Sally, Merrick Morton/Romeo and Juliet); Alastair Miller p.97 (Gout du Noir restaurant), Moviestore p.88 (Brief Encounter); The National Trust Photographic Library/DACS p.130 (Tea in the Hospital/Stanley Spencer); News International/Adrian Sherratt pp.26/27 (exterior Royal Towers of Atlantis); The Orient Express p.18; Pictor pp.10 (3 people talking), 22, 23, 24 (stretch limo, rickshaw, hot air balloon), 34 (person skiing), 49 (Athlete training) 50, 63 (market), 65 (newsagent), 70 (lecture theatre), 95 (Hong Kong, Venice), 99 (VCR); Private Collection pp.132 (The 4th June at Eton with my mother and sisters Morar and Katherine, As SDC to the Governor of Newfoundland, the flight to Le Touquet (Maurice Buxton), Rochdale by-election poster), 133 (Wedding, At Piers Place, Amersham – family sitting on floor, With Bryan Magee before delivering 'Wicked Beyond Belief' to the Home Secretary, With Crummy Carter); Rex Features/Sipa Press pp. 34 (Lou Reed), 35 (Lesley Garrett, David Bowie), 38 (Peter Brooker/Jennifer Lopez, Antonio Banderas), 40 (Nils Jorgensen/Paul McCartney present day), 49 (Ken McKay/Paul McKenna hypnotising, Steve Wood/fashion model), 54 (Richard Gardner/Prison), 88 (Bridget Jones, Sipa/Nana Productions/Annie Hall), 93 (Sipa/Nana Productions/Bill Gates, Nicole Kidman, Dave Pinegar/David Beckham, Charles Sykes/Oprah Winfrey), 129 (Brian Rasic/Venus Williams, Sipa/Nelson Mandela, Ayrton Senna, Ron Sachs/Hillary Clinton, Sipa/Kary H Lasch/Salvador Dali), 148 (Sipa/Diana and Dodi); Chris Rowe p.38 (Chris Rowe); The Royal Towers of Atlantis p.26 (interior); Tim Scott p.107 (DeNica Fairman); The Richard Stone Partnership p.107 (Tyler Butterworth); Tate London, 2002 pp.147 (Hockney – Mr and Mrs Clark and Percy), 149 (Hockney – My Parents); Patience Tomlinson p.107 (Patience Tomlinson); Travel Ink pp.22 (Ron Radkin/elephant, Richard Cuerden/Vietnam), 65 (Stephen Andrews/European kiosk) 66 (Jeremy Phillips/pub N. Yorks), 95 (Geraint Tellem/London, Robin McKelvie/Sydney), 99 (Frances Balham/washing line); Conway van Gelder p.107 (Julia Ford); Vocalpoint p.38 (Lorelei King)

The Publisher and Authors would like to thank the following readers and teachers for their invaluable help with the development of the student's book, listening booklet, and teacher's book material:

Maggie Baigent, Jan Borsbey, Brian Brennan, Jo Cooke, Olivia Date, Richard Frost, Jane Hudson, Amanda Jeffries, Marcel Sanchez, Mike Sayer, Scott Thornbury, Louise Williams.

The Authors would particularly like to thank the following people for their help with the initial research and piloting:

Alastair Banton, Tom Bradbury, Philip Curren, Francis Duncan, Heather Miletto, Louise Porter-Taylor, Lyn and David Scott. Also the teachers at *Edwards School of English, The London School of English, International House*, London, and *Golders Green College of English.*

The Publisher and Authors would also like to thank:

Kenna Bourke for reading and editing the language reference section, Theresa Clementson for reading and editing the teacher's book, Jeff Mohamed and Alan Turner for specific material, Martin Williamson for his enormous contribution to the shaping of the listening material, and to the following actors whose own ideas, anecdotes, and humour are such an important part of the recordings: Gareth Armstrong, Deborah Berlin, Carolyn Bonnyman, Carole Boyd, Lynne Brackley, Jenny Bryce, Tyler Butterworth, Lolita Chacrabati, Jane Collingwood, DeNica Fairman, Elly Fairman, Michael Fenton-Stevens, Julia Ford, William Gaminara, James Goode, Nigel Greaves, Joanna Hall, Jeff Harding, John Hasler, Federay Holmes, Jenny Howe, Frances Jeeter, Jonathan Keeble, Lorelei King, Nick Mercer, Eric Meyers, Richard Mitchley, David Monteith, Cecilia Noble, Paul Panting, Alison Pettitt, Juliet Prague, Marcella Riordan, Chris Rowe, David Shaw-Parker, Gertrude Thomas, Patience Tomlinson, Ralph van Dijk, Clare Wille, James Wilson, Maya Woolfe.